CUNK

— ON —

EVERYTHING

CUNK

— ON —

EVERYTHING

The Encyclopedia Philomena

PHILOMENA CUNK

GRAND
CENTRAL

NEW YORK   BOSTON

Grand Central Publishing
Hachette Book Group
1290 Avenue of the Americas, New York, NY 10104
grandcentralpublishing.com
twitter.com/grandcentralpub

Originally published in hardcover and ebook by Two Roads Books
First U.S. Hardcover Edition: September 2023

Grand Central Publishing is a division of Hachette Book Group, Inc. The Grand
Central Publishing name and logo is a trademark of Hachette Book Group, Inc.

The publisher is not responsible for websites (or their
content) that are not owned by the publisher.

The Hachette Speakers Bureau provides a wide range of authors for
speaking events. To find out more, go to hachettespeakersbureau.
com or email HachetteSpeakers@hbgusa.com.

Grand Central Publishing books may be purchased in bulk for business, educational,
or promotional use. For information, please contact your local bookseller or the
Hachette Book Group Special Markets Department at special.markets@hbgusa.com.

Library of Congress Cataloging-in-Publication Data has been applied for.

ISBNs: 978-1-5387-6676-7 (hardcover), 978-1-5387-6678-1 (ebook)

Printed in the United States of America

LSC-C

Printing 1, 2023

CONTENTS

FOREWORD

By Professor Rupert Delgado, MBE

I'm rather afraid to say that I do not know the author to whom you refer, since I seldom look at the television, but these samples you have sent me are an absolute disgrace. I shall not be contributing a foreword to this book and I am happy for you to quote me on that.

Never contact me again.

PREFACE

By Philomena Cunk

When I was asked to write this book, I remember thinking.

It was a good feeling. And writing this book, that feeling has happened again and again. Thinking is one of the three best things you can do with your brain. I hope that this book will provide "food for thought," which is the scientific word for mind sausages, and maybe go some way to answer all the questions in the universe.

It's hard to know everything, because the world is getting more complicated every day. Maybe in olden times, a caveman would have been able to know everything just by knowing the difference between rocks and food. But someone with that level of knowledge today would be practically unemployable, even in shoe retail.

So how can we know more about the world? One way is through books. Books are like the internet but all in one order and they still work in a tunnel. What you're holding now is a book (unless you've put it down on a table and are holding a cup of tea, in which case what you're holding now is a cup of tea). By reading books, the ideas someone else put in the book travel up your eyes and join your own ideas in your head. It feels weird at first, but I'm told you get used to it.

A lot of books are written by quite boring people you've never heard of, and so never get opened. The best books are written by someone off the television, as the bestseller charts clearly prove. People off the television just write better books, and that's why I'm doing this one. Because otherwise some so-called author might do it instead, and nobody would buy the books and they'd end up in landfill. It's sobering to realize that writing a book and not being off the television can do so much damage to our precious planet.

Think of this book as a helpful guide to the universe, written by someone you trust. Sometimes it's nice to have someone take you by the hand. Sometimes it's not (e.g: if they haven't used the dryer in the bogs for quite long enough, or have been recently gutting a mackerel). But sometimes it's nice to know that someone is going to help you navigate life's more difficult and confusing bits.

You might ask, why me? Well, I've spent the last few years investigating right up the most pressing issues of today and the past in my television series and specials, and I like to think I've been successful at it because that feels nice.

I hope you enjoy learning about everything. I know I have.

Philomena Cunk

Chessington World of Adventures, UK, May 2018

Adam and Eve

The first human to evolve from God was Adam, who was the first man. In those early days, there were no women at all, only men, like on the repeats of *Have I Got News?* on Dave.

This was a problem because the only way to make more Adams was for Adam to have sex with the only other person around: God. I'd imagine God didn't want to mate with Adam because he'd made him in his image, so that's just having sex with yourself, which is weird. Plus you can have sex with yourself anyway, using a wank, and then you get to nod off afterward without any awkward conversation, so God wasn't into that at all. Why should he be? He's God. He can probably have sex with himself a million mysterious ways without needing anyone's help at all. When it comes to having sex with humans, that's more the Holy Ghost's sort of thing for some reason. He's intangible and smooth, like a newly washed duvet cover, so it's probably a "bit of rough" sort of thing. I don't really want to think about it.

Anyway, in order that there could be sex, God made Eve, a woman, who evolved from Adam. Eve came second, like women usually do, but was more evolved. Unlike Adam, whose leaf was just for show, Eve could have babies out her leaf, and so the whole population of Earth was invented.

Eve got in trouble straight away for eating an apple that belonged to God. If he was that fussed about it, he should have put a post-it note on it, like you do in an office fridge. Idiot.

Alexander the Great

Alexander the Great was born in 356 in Ancient Greece and died at the age of 32BC, having become one of the greatest soldiers of all times. He was very much the Andy McNab of his day, only he wasn't just silhouettes. He was also statues.

Alexander rose from nothing, as the son of a simple Greek king, to become the ruler of all of Greece. Then, because that wasn't enough, he invaded literally everywhere that anyone had heard of. At the time, people hadn't heard of many places we take for granted now (America, Chessington World of Adventures, Loompaland) but all the places that had been heard of (basically Greece and the bits next to Greece) fell to Alexander's mighty armies.

Alexander conquered Syria, Persia, Babylonia, India, Turkia, Egyptia, all the places. His soldiers were knackered. They kept falling off their horses, which is why he built a big wooden one called the Trojan Horse that they could ride inside, like a bus, and catch a nap or stare out the window and see what's on top of bus stops. Using this horse he won the Battle of Troy, and beat the Minotaur, which was a bull with the mind of a wasp and the teeth of a duck. To be frank, the Greek myths get a bit confusing here, but he's in most of them. He was so great at fighting that he stopped being a Greek myth and turned into a real boy, like Pinocchio. And that's why we remember him today, if we do.

He was called "the Great" because nobody had invented surnames and they needed a way of telling him apart from the other Alexanders, like Alexander the Drunk and and Alexander the Dog. It looks a bit like he chose his own nickname, though, which is against the rules. He should have let his mates pick one. Though he might just have ended up being called Womble or Piehead or Dr. Spunkwagon or something, and it's harder to conquer the world if you know you're going to have to carve that on all your plinths.

Alexander the Great's was one of the largest empires there had ever been in all of history, which wasn't very long back then. There have been bigger empires since, but that's because things get bigger when they're hot, so there's more world now, thanks to global warming.

Alfred of Great

Alfred of Great was the greatest king England ever had, and we know that because he boasted about his own greatness in his name, like the Notorious B.I.G. or Tom and Barbara Good.

Alfred of Great was a much better king than Ethelred the Unready or Harold The Shit. If we learn anything from this, it's that you should read *all* of a king's name before giving him the job. Alfred basically invented England. Before him, there had been loads of little kingdoms with lots of little kings with Harry Potter names like Eadwig and Eric Bloodaxe. Alfred made one big kingdom called England, from the word "and," meaning "together," and the word "ingle" meaning "fireplace." For some reason. (It's surprising Alfred didn't call his kingdom Alfredland, after what a bighead he'd been about his own name.)

Alfred was called Great because he ran away from his responsibilities and hid in Somerset, stuffing his face and wondering what to do—a proud English tradition that students at Bath University continue to this day.

Despite his bold Vrexit, and his restoration of the city of London, and his legal reforms, and his beefing up the navy and all his many other achievements, Alfred is most famous for not helping with some burnt cakes. In that respect, he was very much the Sue Perkins of his day.

..................................🦆..................................

Alphabet

The alphabet is in that order because that's the order the letters were invented in. You can tell that because all the boring ones like B and A are at the front and all the exciting futuristic space ones like X and Z are at the back. Z is sort of the iPhone X of the alphabet.

Some countries have banned some of the alphabet. In Italy, the letter W is illegal. And in Hawaii, they only have twelve letters, because it's not a very big place. This is why the word "Hawaii" has such a funny ending—because there's no Y available to help get across that the name means "like a Hawai."

Some languages have different alphabets. Russia's alphabet

is all the same letters but in a mirror. The Arabic alphabet is all beautiful eyebrows. Chinese is mainly piles of sticks.

The only alphabet that's in the right order is the alphabet of numbers, which goes from one, which is the smallest, all the way up to 0, which is smaller. And with those ten digits you can count almost anything, except time, which is in twelves.

Alt Right, The

There's this group of people called the "alt right," which is, like, a pun on "all right," but because they're really *not* all right, they're called "alt right." They could have been called the "all wrong" but that sounds LITERALLY all wrong. They're like if LBC wanted its own country.

Some people say the alt right are Neo-Nazis, but they're not, because they haven't got uniforms or mustaches and don't all walk at the same speed. They're as different from the Nazis as Starburst are to Opal Fruits.

The alt right are the *alternative right*. You'd think alternative meant "different" but in this case it means "exactly the same but worse." Like if you asked for an alternative to sprouts and some-one served you sprouts in sick.

They say really outrageous things, like they're drunk, but without the bit the next day where they've got a headache and try to take it all back. They want more space for themselves and people like them, which is why a lot of them are fat. To claim more room. And they don't like people who aren't like them. Black people. Muslim people. Hispanic people. Gay people. Woman people. They fight for white rights and men's rights, which is why it was a big deal when they finally managed to get a white man to be president.

They probably also got their name from that thing you do on a computer to turn it off and turn it on again, which is what they want to do with the planet.

.... 🦆 ....

Anglo-Saxons

One of the great mysteries of history is: who were the Anglo-Saxons? If you ask a historian, they'll tell you, but you probably won't be listening.

The Anglo-Saxons seemed to come from nowhere, and disappear almost straight away, yet still be all around us, like the band Texas. And they're famous for almost nothing, like the band Texas. They didn't have togas or longboats or the Battle of Hastings. They didn't have mountain-top cities or pyramids or gladiators. They were almost completely unmemorable and ordinary and a bit boring, like the band Texas. You wouldn't really know they were there. And that's why England is named after them.

What we do know about the Anglo-Saxons is that they were a very pissed off lot, because they invented all the more interesting swearwords we still use today, including sard, scitan and rastagr. But the Anglo-Saxons didn't write much down, because the Romans took all the pens with them when they left Britain, and the Angles went a bit odd and starting making up whatever rubbish came into their heads, and soon people were banging on about monsters, and **King Arthur**, and wizards and dragons. In fact, the only trustworthy written accounts we have of this time are the adventures of Bilbo Baggins.

But add it all up and it sort of makes sense: the swearing, the making stuff up, the short shelf life, not going out much, the love of stories about goblins and dragons—it's pretty clear that the Anglo-Saxons were the first ever trolls. In fact, you can bet that if the Anglo-Saxons had been on Twitter today, it would be exactly like it already is.

Animals

Animals is what we call anything that's alive that isn't a plant or a tree or a person or a fire or a virus or a volcano or a bush. It's a pretty big collection, so we humans (I'm sort of assuming you, the reader, aren't a dog or a robot) have done the sensible thing and given each animal a different name. So a bird is called a bird. Except then you have to get specific because not all birds are the same. So a jay is different from a tit. Except not all tits are the same. So a great tit is different from a blue tit. Except not all blue tits are the same. So an African blue tit is different from an Eurasian blue tit. And it all gets a bit too fiddly, and there's too many of them, and they've all got names in Latin or medicine or something, so let's cut to the chase and just concentrate on the important ones.

DUCKS

Ducks are the only fish who swim on the top part of the water. They are also the only fish with feathers. You might think swans would count, but swans are not fish, like ducks, they're sort of big boil-washed pigeons. Ducks can also be eaten by anyone, unlike swans who can only be eaten by the Queen. If a normal human tries to eat a swan, they die, because swan meat is too royal to be digested by commoners. But the Queen has a special stomach for digesting swan, where the swan meat is tenderized using a load of jewels she swallows every day for just this purpose—like reptiles and birds do when they eat stones.

When a duck swims along the top of the water, there appears to be another duck underneath it, upside down. But this isn't an actual duck, it's a mirror of a duck. Even though everything in a mirror is backward, the mirror duck swims in the same direction as the actual duck. This is because if a mirror duck went a different way to its actual duck, different ducks' reflections could get mixed up, and a duck might be a mallard on top but a coot underneath, which would make bird-watching almost impossible.

In winter, ducks fly south to where the weather is warmer. They know which way is south by looking at the V-shape lots of them make when they fly in the sky and following the pointy end. Ducks lay eggs, like all fish.

INSECTS

Insects are the smallest creatures in the world, and mainly look like punctuation with legs. Humans don't have much use for insects, unlike other animals, because they're too small to ride, and it's hard to get enough of them in one place to turn into a roast dinner.

All insects have four legs. They also have two arms. Some of them have wings, usually an even number of them, to stop them flying round in circles, although moths somehow manage it anyway. Maybe they've got something heavy in one pocket.

Everyone agrees that the worst insects are flies, and the best ones are butterflies. You can make most things better by adding butter (mashed potato, fried bread, Wotsits, etc.). Flies walk around in animal shit and then come into your kitchen and stand in your food. It's as if Chris Packham came round and lowered himself into your soup, boots-first. If Chris Packham did that, he shouldn't be surprised if you ran after him, trying to smash his brains in with a plastic spatula, but flies get really cross about it. They're complete pricks.

Caterpillars are like insects, except they're more like a haunted sleeping bag. They eat constantly, mostly leaves, chocolate cake, ice cream cones, pickles, Swiss cheese, salami, lollipops, cherry pie, sausages, cupcakes and watermelon. Then they turn into a beautiful chrysalis. Sadly, soon after, the chrysalis is usually torn apart by a butterfly, the natural predator of the chrysalis, before it can fly away or lay its eggs.

Moths are like the BBC4 version of butterflies—a bit more boring, and mainly on at night. They sleep during the day, but once it is dark, they hunt in packs for their chief food: light-bulbs. The moths surround the lightbulb, and attack it, by flying repeatedly into it for hours on end until the lightbulb becomes exhausted and drops to the ground. One of the great-est sights in nature is a pride of moths dragging a subdued lightbulb back to their nest to feed to their moth cubs. Unfortunately, because this happens at night, nobody has ever seen it. Even David Attenborough has to get some kip in now and again.

The smallest insect is the ant. Ants gather together in huge gangs and build hills to make themselves appear bigger so they don't get bullied by bigger insects like beetles and octopuses. One ant can carry up to 5,000 times its own weight, but the webpage I found this fact on didn't say which ant.

The most magical and mysterious of all the insects is the bee. Bees turn flowers into honey by rubbing their legs on the flowers and then going into a little house. It's not clear how they do it. It could be a trick, because it's all done behind closed doors, which is a bit suspicious.

Think about it

Is it possible that the bees just buy honey from the shops? Maybe they all swarm together into a human shape and then get inside a long coat so nobody knows it's them and go down Asda. They then probably hide the honey in the little house, so no one can see the jars, and bring some of it out when a human comes to see if they've turned the flowers into honey by rubbing their legs on them (which is quite an unlikely story when you think about it).

There have been insects on Earth much longer than humans, but they've not really done much. Sometimes you get the feeling they're just wasting their time. Scientists reckon that insects will be around long after humans have gone, so maybe they could get off their arses then.

SNAILS

You can't trust snails. They're just slugs disguised as the seaside.

TIGERS

Tigers are the biggest of the big cats except for lions, who, it turns out, because I stopped just then and looked it up, are slightly smaller, so tigers are the biggest and I shouldn't have said lions. But if I hadn't said lions I wouldn't have looked it up and I wouldn't know that fact about tigers, whatever it was, so you live and learn.

Tigers are the ones who look like an orange barcode with teeth. They live in India and Russia and Chessington World of Adventures and eat deer, buffaloes and Frosties.

At the beginning of the 20th century, there were around 100,000 tigers in the wild, but that number has fallen to around 3,000, because tigers are really dangerous and if you've got 100,000 of them wandering about, something has to be done. It's a real success story for the human race.

Nowadays, there are more tigers in zoos and rap videos and magic shows than in the wild, which is safer, unless you're whichever one of Siegfried and Freud it was who got his face bitten off. In the wild, tigers tend to eat more meat and less Frosties. It's important to feed your tiger enough Frosties to stop him biting your head off, a lesson that either Siegfried or Freud learned tragically too late.

Tigers are intelligent. In captivity tigers can be taught to do tricks like jumping through a hoop of fire or saying that certain products are "grrrreeat," like one of the most famous advertising tigers of all time, Tiger Woods.

Archeology

Archeology is the science of finding things that people in the past hid in the ground. Nobody knows why people in the past buried their stuff. Maybe they were worried that burglars might steal it, but some of the stuff they buried was rubbish, like loads of flint arrowheads and bits of shoe.

It's possible that the stuff was buried in a hurry, so they didn't really check what it was, and buried everything they could get their hands on, because someone up a castle had spotted that loads of burglars were coming. What with pirates and highwaymen and Robin Hoods all over the place, in them days you couldn't trust anyone with anything unless it was nailed down, and even then they might nick the nails and bury them.

Some people, like the Romans, even buried themselves in the ground using volcanoes. Even though it remains a mystery why people buried things (including themselves) under the ground, the fact that they did has helped us understand what people were like in the past: a bit mad, and keen on burying stuff. Without all the burying, history would only be words people wrote down, and that would make it more boring, because you would have to read about an old crown, rather than being able to put it on your head and swan about in it, like I imagine archeologists are doing all the time.

The most famous archeologists of all time are Tony Robinson and Indiana Jones. The interesting thing about Tony Robinson and Indiana Jones is that they both either wear that hat, or have a mate who wears that hat. It's one of the stand-out features of archeology, that hat. It's why if an archeologist loses his hat, he has to dive back into the collapsing temple to rescue it, like Tony Robinson's mate is doing all the time.

The only people who still bury stuff these days, really, are dogs. Maybe this is proof that the people of the past used to be dogs. If we keep digging, we may find that crucial piece of evidence that proves that everyone in the past was a dog. Maybe somewhere, under the ground, are loads of bones. But sadly, until someone digs up an old bone, this thing about everyone being a dog in the olden days will have to stay nothing but a theory. Science is a harsh mistress.

Archie Medes

Archie Medes was the cleanest of the Greek philosophers. He lived in a bath, and showed off all the time about how much cleaner he was than Plato and the other philosophers who just did a quick face, front and forks with a Greek flannel, which was probably called a phlannel. He'd point at them and say they smelled. "You reeker," he'd shout. Which became his catchphrase.

Eventually (probably when he got out of the bath) Archie Medes noticed that when he got out of the bath, the water went down. That was because he'd pulled the plug out. Nobody had ever pulled the plug out of a bath before, they'd just poured more hot water in, until it overflowed, and soon Archie had become known as the father of bathematics, the science of baths.

Archie Medes also discovered that water goes the other way out of a bath in Australia (up out of the plughole and back into the bath, because the country is upside down) and that if you stay too long in the bath, your toes go weird.

Unanswered Questions about Baths

💀 If you stayed in a bath for weeks, would you go so wrinkly that you got old?

💀 Why didn't the other things in the bathroom get the room named after them? Why isn't it "the toiletroom" or "the sinkroom" or "the toothbrushroom"?

Architecture

For centuries of millennia, man lived outdoors, hunting deer and nuts. Then one day, it must of rained, and man discovered a new place: indoors. And it was here he made his biggest discovery since he discovered indoors: architecture.

Architecture is posh for "buildings." And buildings are all around us, expecially when we're inside them. So why are buildings? Animals don't have buildings, except zoos or the top bit of a snail. But humans do.

Before architecture, there was caves. You didn't build a cave, you just found it. And sometimes it was full of bears, which made it hard to put up wallpaper. So man needed somewhere else to live. He tried living in clothes, but they weren't thick enough. So he started building buildings called buildings. Buildings don't just grow out of the ground, like flowers or lamp-posts. They have to be made by someone—and that someone is an architect. Learning to turn into an architect takes seven years, which is even longer than it takes to turn into a wizard.

Some of the oldest buildings were Stonehenge, the Pyramids and St. Paul Cathedral. St. Paul Cathedral was architected by Sir Christopher Robin. It was made to replace the old one which had been burned down in the Great Fire, which was lucky or there wouldn't have been room. It's regarded as significant by architects because it has the biggest tit of any building in the world. You can even go up in the tit today, though you have to whisper so it sounds like you're taking it seriously.

There are all different words for the fashions in architecture. St. Paul's is Brock. Another style is Goth. Goth architecture is all castles and is mainly for Frankingsteins. It's meant to frighten you. Even Notre Dame, France's most important church, is Goth. And that's because French God is more frightening than British God, because he smokes.

Art Deco came after Brock, and is the word for buildings off Batman, and Cheese and Wooster. It's all got round bits on it and looks like a boat, but a concrete boat. When the Art Decos tried to sail a building, that was *Titanic*. And literally millions died.

In War Two, Hitler dropped loads of bombs on Britain, killing lots of the architecture and forcing cockneys to go and live in tubes. Britain needed rebuilding, like a dropped Lego set, and architects decided to do it differently. New styles were tried out, like high-rise buildings.

High-rise buildings were controversial at first, until it was decided that they were a good way to pile poor people in the sky, out of the way. Some of these buildings are considered ugly these days, but others are considered to be hideous eyesores. The national National Theatre is one. It's designed to be so ugly that people are glad to be inside watching boring plays. It's in an architecture called Brutalism, which means punching, and is why it looks like a skinhead.

For a long time, we built buildings you could see. But then buildings got so ugly it was best they were see-through to stop people complaining, so we made them just of glass. Then, in the year 9/11, two airplanes bumped into some tall glass buildings because they couldn't see them, and some people started to wonder whether tall buildings were such a good idea at all. The answer was yes. So we've built loads more.

The Shard is the biggest piece of glass in the world. It's even bigger than the windows at Debenhams, or the sea. It's over a thousand feet tall, and goes to a point. It can't be any taller than that, because a thousand feet up is where the sides meet. Any taller and it would start going out again, like a big bow-tie, and then they'd have to build another London, upside down, at the top, which would be too expensive. There's some restaurant on the fifty-second floor of the Shard. All the food has to be brought up here in lifts, which means you can go there and eat the highest potato in Britain.

Buildings used to have stuff all over them that made them interesting, and be made of things you can see, like bricks, but now they're like sort of fishtanks made of graph paper and you can't remember where they are, or if you're in one.

In the future, buildings might even be so advanced that they're invisible, and when people go up stairs they'll look like they're going to heaven. Who knows, with skyscrapers all over the world getting taller and taller, one might even reach heaven. And one day, we might be able to sit in the top floor restaurant and eat our soup with an amazing view—of God.

> **Unanswered Questions about Architecture**
>
> 🐚 Is the underneath of a floor always a ceiling? Could you have a floor with a wall on the other side?
>
> 🐚 How do you enter your street for a Postcode Lottery?
>
> 🐚 Are bus stops the only buildings with one wall?

Art

Art is the scientific word for paintings. A painting is a way of making castles and hills and kings and pineapples in bowls into a flat rectangle that's easier to hang on a wall than a real castle or pineapple.

The first art was paintings of cows in caves. The cows didn't live in the caves, so when cavemen wanted to look at a really good cow, and it was cold outside or raining, they needed to do one on the wall, which was nearly as good, but not quite. This is where the idea of art not being quite as good as the real thing comes from, and you can see this to this day. For example, if you try and eat the painting of an orange on the label of a jar of marmalade, it doesn't taste anywhere near as good as a real orange, it tastes of paper, and that's art.

The best artists are the ones who can nearly make you think the thing in the painting is a real one. It's a trick, like Dynamo might do, but it's basically a lie. People don't like liars, which is why most artists earn no money and eventually starve to death.

MICHAEL ANGELO

The first artist to work out how to do bums properly was Michael Angelo. He did loads of bums and was even asked to paint bums on the roof of the Pope's house. That's Catholics for you.

LEONARD DA VINCI

Leonard Da Vinci did the most famous painting that has ever been done, a portrait of a lady called Mona Lisa. The painting now belongs to the French, who keep it in the loo, where her enigmatic smile puts French people at their ease when they're shitting into the floor, like they do.

He also invented the helicopter, but nobody worked it out because he did it in his famous code, which couldn't be cracked by anyone until they worked out it was backward. Helicopters built without decoding the code would not only have been made of old-fashioned stuff like turnips and haystacks, but thanks to the Da Vinci Code, would also have been the wrong way up, and would only fly tail-first, downwards, probably with the twirly bits staying still and the cabin spinning round like mad. By the time renowned author Dan Brown cracked the Da Vinci Code it was too late and the helicopter had been invented already and even Noel Edmonds had one, so it wasn't such a big deal.

VINCENT VAN GOGH

Vincent Van Gogh (pronounced "Van Guff") was so bad at painting that he cut off his own ear, which is hard with a paintbrush. He must have been waving it about quite hard, and if you've seen some of his paintings that does make a lot of sense. It was a mad thing to do because it wasn't his ear's fault that he was shit at painting. It was his hands'. He never sold a single painting to anyone in his lifetime, and they were never made into a book or a tea towel, which is tragic, because even Prince Charles managed that, and his are frankly appalling.

ANDY WARHOLE

Andy Warhole changed the world of art by painting with soup. This gave him only five colors: tomato, chicken, oxtail, winter vegetable and carrot-and-coriander. When he did a painting of the actor Marilyn Monroe, he gave her a winter vegetable face, which was quite shocking for the time because films were in black and white and nobody knew. David Bowie wrote a song about Andy Warhole called "Scary Monsters and Souper Creeps," because of all the soup.

TONY HART

After Andy Warhole, the most important artist was probably Tony Hart, who did paintings of harbors at sunset in chalk by enchanting a clay man to help him. Tony Hart was sadly eventually destroyed by the dark magic that had gained him his fame, and died, tragically, every year or so, on Twitter.

GRAYSON PERRY

Most painters are dead, but one of the most modern painters still alive today is the painter Grayson Perry. She won a famous art prize by painting using pots. People had painted using pots before, but they'd usually just dipped their brushes in them to get the paint out. Grayson revolutionized art by putting the pots themselves on display, and soon had a television series where she disguised herself as a man, which again, really turned eyebrows.

Astronomy

Our planet is not the only one in the universe. There are loads of others, apparently.

There are planets we all know, like Earth, and the sandy one Darth Vader's from and the Moon. But there are millions of planets we've never even seen, and are unlikely to ever visit, but which scientists won't stop banging on about.

Some of these planets may be able to support life, but we've already got one of those and it's much closer, so looking for other planets humans can live on is a bit like being married to someone you get on with perfectly well and then wasting all evening not talking to them and staring at Tinder.

The planets that orbit our sun are the closest ones, and these are known as "the solero system" because some of them are freezing cold and look a bit like ice cream.

There used to be nine planets in the solero system, but scientists recently found out they'd made a cock-up and one of them, Pluto, was not a planet after all, but Mickey Mouse's dog.

It's hard to know how scientists could make such a basic mistake, but telescopes don't just look into the sky, you can also use them to look through a neighbor's window, so maybe they'd pointed their telescopes at a cartoon on next door's TV instead, and then they were too embarrassed to admit they'd not been gazing into the sky but had been trying to spy on a lady in a bra. I imagine it gets lonely in an observatory.

The smallest planet in the solero system is Mercury but nobody lives there, so if you moved there it would feel surprisingly roomy, at least compared to somewhere like Coventry. The biggest planet is Jupiter, which is huge and swollen and blotchy, like it's just had a full roast dinner with all the trimmings, and mainly gas, like it went for the vegetarian option.

The best planet is probably Anus. Anus used to be called Uranus but so many people made rude jokes about it that scientists gave up and just said "you go for it," like when James Blunt finally accepted he had become rhyming slang and would be better just laughing it off.

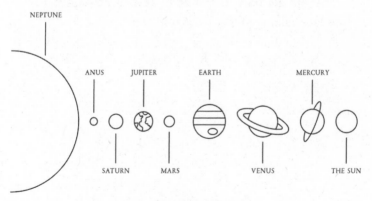

The Solero System

You might think our closest planet is the Moon. But you'd be wrong. Because our closest planet is Earth. Earth is the science name for the world, so it has two names, like Puff Daddy and everything in Wales.

It's almost impossible to believe that the world that you live on isn't just a world, but also a planet, flying through space at enormous speed. It's enough to make you throw up. That's probably why scientists wear white coats—so they can keep their cardigans clean of vomit.

No human has ever visited another planet, except the Moon, and even then they did it on Earth using actors. And that's because visiting another planet is impossible.

Why it's impossible to visit other planets

 easyJet don't go there.

 Not enough gravity. You'd need to pack your own.

 Far awayness.

 There's no food when you get there.

 Spain is nicer than Space.

Atoms

People used to think that the smallest things were stuff like peas and ants, but inside even the smallest pea are literally dozens of smaller things called atoms. Different atoms make different things, which is why a pea is different than an ant, even if they might look the same from an airplane.

Inside everything in the world and space is atoms. The only thing that isn't made of atoms is space itself, which is made of nothing. Scientists testimate that there is more nothing in the universe than there is stuff. Which is why it's so amazing that I can't fit any more in my sock drawer.

Atoms are like little balls and sticks, like a sort of shit Lego they had in the war that your granddad might bang on about. Atoms are too small to see with the naked eye, so you need to make your eye not naked by wearing a microscope on it like a hat. If you look down the microscope (hat) you can see the balls and sticks (atoms), and that's the simplest way to understand how everything works.

Atoms are the smallest things that there are or can be, except for the smaller things that are inside atoms, apparently. I mean, FFS.

The things inside the atoms are called nucleuses, electrions and protein. They are so tiny you couldn't even pick them up if you licked your finger and dabbed at them like sherbet. The rest of the atom, which is most of it, is more nothing. On average, when you think about it, that means every thing is mainly nothing, so it's surprising all the fuss that's made about shoplifting.

Scientists can't leave well alone so some of them tried to break atoms open to see what was inside. And what's inside was a huge mushroom, which nobody expected. The mushrooms can be used to destroy cities and cause Godzillas, but can also run power stations that sometimes don't even explode.

Atoms-powered power stations don't create as much mess as the old ones that use coal, because atoms aren't covered in that black stuff. It's a hard truth that if we want to keep our kettles and hair straighteners boiling hot, we are going to have to make friends with atoms, and not mind the occasional Godzilla. It is a small price to pay, when you think about it, not much bigger than an atom itself. But much smaller than a Godzilla. They're massive.

"Auld Lang Syne"

"Auld Lang Syne" is a nonsense rhyme we all sing on New Year's Eve. By the time it gets near to midnight, everybody's so trolleyed that they can't remember the words to any real song, so it's easier to just sing a load of gibberish.

It's also got a really easy dance, which involves crossing your arms and doing really businessy handshakes with the people either side of you. You don't even have to move your legs. It's easier than the conga. And there's less chance of someone going for your bum.

....🦆..

Australia

Australia is a country on the other side of the world where everything happens upside down and back to front, so the whole place is topsy-turvy. Unlike the rest of the world, they have Christmas in the summer, eat their dinner outdoors and like talking to Australians.

Australia's chief industry is spiders. Other countries have to import dangerous animals, but Australia makes all its own, which is handy because it's so far away that if they had to order their poisonous snakes from Amazon, they'd be dead by the time the package arrived.

Australia has invented loads of animals, like the kangaroo, the koala and the barbecue, but none of them has caught on in other countries, except the barbecue. Sadly all the wild barbecues were hunted to extinction hundreds of years ago by hungry sailors, and now the only ones you see are robot ones, made out of metal and bricks.

Australia was originally colonized by thieves covered in soot from big cities like London. They were sent there in big ships, in the hope that loads of sunshine and beer would teach them a bloody good lesson. But as soon as the criminals landed, they stole a whole country, which was a much bigger crime than nicking a cabbage or whatever they'd gone down for, proving that if you trap criminals with loads of other criminals, it only makes them worse.

One place you always see Australians is everywhere. They travel a lot, because the only thing they love more than being in Australia is telling people how much they love being in Australia, and the best place to talk about how much better Australia is than everywhere else is somewhere a long way from Australia, so that the person you're telling can't pop into Australia and check if it's any good or whether you're talking a load of koalashit.

Australia is so far away that even the parts of Australia that are actually in Australia are far away from each other. This is why Australians are amongst the friendliest people on Earth: because they've never met each other.

Famous Australians include Skippy the Bush Kangaroo,

Dannii Minogue and Adolf Hitler. Even though Hitler was king of Germany, he was actually not born in Germany at all, but Australia, in a small town on the German-Australian border. He said it was really important to know where people come from, but that just proves that it isn't.

Bacon, Francis

Sir Francis Bacon was one of the most all-round clever people who has ever lived. He did more different things than most of us can dream of.

He was an English statesman, philosopher and Irish painter, who lived at the time of Elizabeth I and Elizabeth II. He not only became Lord Chancellor in 1618, but still found time to write one of the first science books in 1620, and, after a short rest, painted the painting *Three Studies For Figures At The Base Of The Crucifixion* in 1944.

Some people believe he had a hand in writing Shakespeare's plays, and his portrait of Lucien Freud, painted in 1969, when he was 408 years old and drunk, is one of the most expensive ever sold. He did so many things that he is one of the few historical English/Irish figures to require two completely different and contradictory Wikipedia pages.

Ballet

Ballet is like dancing, but you don't do it yourself, someone else does it, which is the main difference between ballet and The Hokey Cokey. There are some other dances which are just watched rather than done yourself, like Riverdance, but ballet is different because you not only don't do it, you don't watch it either. Nobody does, except a few really posh people, and they might be lying.

I don't think even the Queen really watches ballet, because she gets worn out watching dancing all day for work. Every time she visits a country, they do a dance she has to sit through with a face like a bulldog watching ballet. So the last thing she wants is to watch dances in her spare time. I don't blame her.

The women in ballet have their hair up in really tight scrunchies, and the men wear tight leggings, so you can see their cobblers, which I think must explain a lot of the appeal. It's always nice to see a load of cobblers in a row. Although, because ballet is dead posh, the men dancers don't come on dressed as firemen, put on a bit of Tom Jones, strip their leggings off and throw them at hen parties. It's a lot more boring than that.

Even though nobody likes ballet, it still exists, like yellow Quality Streets and *Antiques Roadshow.* It's paid for not by people wanting to see it, but from money raised by scratchcards, so that ballerinas don't die out, like the snow leopard nearly did just because nobody wanted to see it. Often ballets are about endangered creatures, like swans, so maybe they could do one about snow leopards, and poor people could save the planet, through scratchcards.

Battle of Hastings, The

The most famous battle in British history apart from the Battle of Britain (which the town of Battle, near Hastings, is named after) is the Battle of Hastings.

The year is 1066. (It isn't any more, but you have to pretend it is to tell the story, apparently.) Britain is invaded by William of Normandy and his huge army, bringing their French cuisine and their Norman wisdom. William thinks he should be king of England, even though he's French. And King Harold of England thinks William should be dead, even though he's alive. The two sides just can't agree, so they agree to fight it out in a miniature war called a battle.

On Saturday 14th October, they meet in a field and start smashing each other to bits. The English are the home side, with all the advantages that brings, but it soon becomes clear the French are much better at war. They've got better weapons, and these sort of giant dog-monsters called horses.

You can still visit the field where the battle happened today, although these days it's just a field. You can't visit the battle, because it's stopped now, because the year isn't 1066, as I explained earlier. Though I'd completely understand if you're confused, because I said it was 1066. I'm with you there. I wish I hadn't done it now. I'll have to look at a calendar now, or I'll keep thinking it's 1066 and I'll go to all my 1066 appointments rather than the ones I've actually got today. Bloody hell, it's a minefield. Not the one where the Battle of Hastings happened. That wasn't a minefield. Or it'd have been over quicker.

But anyway, back in 1066 (not now), Harold stages a comeback, and is the first to win when he triumphantly catches an arrow in his eye, the kind of fuck-you show-off act of soldiering that really rallies an army behind someone. Sadly it isn't enough, and he dies soon after. No one knows why.

The next person to win is William. At last his nickname, William the Conqueror, makes sense. And William celebrates his victory by changing everything into French, like you can do on Google these days without battle-axing anyone to death, and that's progress.

He renames all the meat after French. Cow becomes beef (*boeuf*), sheep becomes mutton (*mouton*) and hen becomes chicken (*chicane*). He introduces lots of new French ideas, like blouses, wealth and mustaches. He bungs up lots of French churches and cathedrals that stand to this day, amazingly all built by just one man, a genius called Norman Architecture. In just a few decades, England has become a sort of giant exchange trip, except without the fourteen hours on a coach eating nothing but Skips and the clumsy kiss with some oniony boy called Philippe because your best mate got Didier, the good-looking one.

THE BAYWATCH TAPESTRY

So how do we know all this detail about the Battle of Hastings? Well, we've got an accurate visual record of the whole thing thanks to a quick-thinking bystander, who took a tapestry of it.

Despite looking like a *Games of Throne* season finale drawn by an eight-year-old, the Baywatch Tapestry captures the full force of the battle. It's just like being there, but in wool. You can see French archers steaming in on their blue horses. You can see sort of stick fights. You can see some chopped up people and goose monsters and a sort of lion thing eating its own tail. It's an amazing historical artifact, and it's also one of the few photographs made of string.

Beatles, Them

In Britain in the 1950s and 1960s, everything and everyone and everything was gray and had buttons on it. But all that was about to change thanks to four boys from Liverpool: George, Ringo and their guitarists. A pop band called Them Beatles.

These Beatles didn't have six legs. They had eight legs, like on a spider. Everywhere they went, girls screamed, like with a spider. But unlike spiders, the Beatles never crawled into anyone's mouth when they were asleep. Instead they sang— which scientists still claim spiders don't, in spite of my findings.

Them Beatles started from humble beginnings. In the early days they couldn't afford individual haircuts, and had to copy and paste the same one onto each of their heads. But their catchy jingles were so infectious, they soon led to an epidemic called "Beatlemania." And Them Beatles wanted to hold your hand, which only made the disease spread faster. Soon it spread across the Atlantic, to America, a country which was still there.

While Them Beatles were in the USA they started to become influenced by the Hippies—who were sort of American wombles. They experimented with a drug called LSD which made the user see and hear things that weren't really happening—a bit like

Netflix or Derren Brown. As a result, their music turned psychopathic.

Psychopathic drugs made Them Beatles stop singing simple songs about love and cars, and start writing about things that went a lot deeper, like submarines.

And Them Beatles discovered something that had long been lacking in Britain: color. They found yellow first, then the other ones. And almost overnight (which means not overnight), Britain went from gray to groovy. Suddenly it was cool to ignore society and just be whoever you wanted to be, as long as you had long hair and flamboyant clothing like everybody else. Ringo, George and their guitarists all grew long hair and beards, and sort of sprouted, like it was spring and all Them Beatles were suddenly coming into bloom.

Sadly, Them Beatles came to a sorry end. Far from their heyday, performing for thousands of screaming fans in enormous stadiums, their last gig was on a grotty rooftop, to an audience of just a handful of people. It was 1969, and for some reason it really felt like the 60s was nearly over.

Beeps

Beeps are the sound of the modern world. Everywhere you go today, there's beeps.

Your phone beeps to wake you up. The smoke alarm is beeping because the battery needs changing. You make a cup of tea and the kettle beeps to tell you the water's boiled. The microwave beeps to tell you your Weetabix has cooked. The burglar alarm beeps on the way out of the flat. Your phone beeps to tell you you've got a WhatsApp notification. The cash machine beeps. The doors on the bus beep. You go through the ticket barrier at the railway station and it beeps. The train doors beep. Your phone beeps to tell you someone's left the WhatsApp group chat. The pedestrian crossing beeps. A van beeps to tell you it's turning right. Your pass beeps on the way into the office. Your computer beeps when you start it up. Your phone beeps to tell you you've got a Tinder notification. The coffee machine in the kitchen beeps. The aircon remote beeps. You walk into a shop and it beeps. You walk out of a shop with a shirt with the tag still on it and it beeps. Someone swears on the news and they beep it. Beeps, beeps, beeps, all day and everywhere.

Pretty much the only thing that doesn't beep these days is shoes, and beeping shoes can only be a few years off. As far as the next generation's concerned, they've already got lights on.

But beeps haven't always been around. Before beeps, there was only dings and booms, and even booms were rare. Every now and then, you'd hear a nice little ding from a phone or a doorbell or something, but other than that it was just birdsong and factories. We didn't need to be constantly notified that doors were opening and water was boiled and switches had been switched and Greg from Basildon thinks you're 1 PIECE OF SMOKIN HOT ASS!!!

Whoever's making all these beeps is making a fortune. Yet you never hear about the world's beep billionaires. Maybe they're a shadowy group of international beepspeople who meet in secret to discuss what else they can add beeps to. What'll it be this year? Taps that beep when you turn them on? Sunglasses that beep to let you know you're blinking? Sandwiches that beep when you bite into them? Are they genetically engineering bees that beep rather than buzz? It's proper Frankingstein science.

One day, we're going to have to think seriously about the consequences of all this beeping. What happens if they get into the sea and start threatening marine life? Science must prioritize biodegradable beeps, or the planet might be beeped to death.

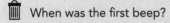

Unanswered Questions about Beeps

🗑 When was the first beep?

🗑 Do the machines that make the things that go beep go beep?

🗑 Why are there no really low beeps?

🗑 What's the difference between a beep and a bleep?

Belgium

You may not have heard of Belgium, but apparently it is the country between Germany and France that invented the bun. Even though France and Germany are more famous, Belgium still definitely exists, and paperwork from Eurocrats in Brussels proves it. Even they believe in Belgium.

The earliest evidence for Belgium came when the first Eurostar train arrived at Waterloo, carrying people claiming to be from there. There are also references to it in the French cartoon *Tintin*. Famous French people who have visited Belgium include Adolphe O'Phone, inventor of the saxophone, and the French karate champion Jean Claude Van Damme.

People in Belgium speak either Dutch or French but not Belgian, which is a language that has never been invented. But there's a good reason for that: the Belgians invented chips. And once you've invented chips, you've frankly peaked. Nothing will ever be invented that's better than chips—not even a language —so the Belgians stopped there. And had some chips.

Big Bang, The

Imagine a time before everything. Like when you wake up at 4 a.m for a wee, but worse.

In the beginning there was nothing. And not just a little bit of nothing. Loads of it. All over the place. Which there wasn't, because there wasn't a place. There wasn't even time. Imagine a time before time. (Except it wasn't technically "before," because it was before beforeness.)

Some people think it's hard to imagine nothing, but I find it very easy. Imagine an orange. Now imagine it's not there. Now do that with everything.

But before there was everything, there was nothing. Empty. Timeless. Without motion. Or energy. Or hope. Like parts of Plymouth.

Then, finally, there was something, and it was called the Big Bang. It might sound like a complicated scientific idea, but it comes from the word "Big," meaning big, and the word "Bang," meaning something that goes bang.

The Big Bang was where everything started. And to be honest, it's nice to have something to blame. What was it like? Nobody knows. Because nobody was there to see it. Like *Top Gear* when it went to Amazon. It was probably deafening—although ears didn't exist, so we can't be sure—and probably looked spectacular—although eyes didn't exist, so it doesn't matter.

The Big Bang was an explosion, but instead of destroying stuff, it made more stuff, like when you try and close a window on a mucky website and it just makes loads more little windows and you can't stop it.

The Big Bang, a bit like *The Big Bang Theory*, made stars of its main players, except the main players in the Big Bang were atoms. Atoms that would one day be understood by people like the clever men in *The Big Bang Theory*. *The Big Bang Theory* is named after the Big Bang theory, which is named after the Big Bang. The theory (not the *Theory*) says that there was a big bang, and was first proposed by a Catholic priest in the 1920s. Priests these days have to be careful about proposing any sort of bangs because they might be misunderstood for perverts.

A lot of the work on the Big Bang theory was done by an astrologer called Edwin Bubble, who noticed that galaxies were running away from us, probably in case we all went bang again. The Bubble telescope is named after him. But the term "Big Bang" was first used by Fred Hoyle, a scientist who didn't believe in the Big Bang, which is a bit like R.E.M. not liking "Shiny Happy People" even though it was their own stupid fault in the first place.

There are still people who don't believe in the Big Bang, like people who believe the Earth was made in six days by a bored God. But even then, some religious people think God might have made the Big Bang. But if he had, it would have been mentioned in the Bible. After all, it's a much more exciting opening than "Once upon a time there was the word," which is how it kicks off now.

Boffins at the Large Hadron Colander have recently made a little Big Bang called a primordial soup. If you ask me, making soup out of the most expensive machine in the world is a waste of money. You can get a soupmaker from Argos for £39.99. It's probably because they're boffins that they have to overcomplicate things. And boffins are rubbish in the kitchen. Everybody knows that. They have things like bread on toast.

Black Death, The

The Black Death wasn't anywhere near as much fun as it sounds, and it sounds like absolutely no fun at all. That's how awful it was. Like, if you had the word "death" and you thought, "No, not nearly awful enough: how can I make this much worse?" you might put the word "black" in front of it. Same as if you had the word "leftovers" and put the word "value" in front of it. It'd really ruin your sales.

The Black Death was a plague. Not a metaphorical plague like a metaphorical plague, but an actual plague—made of plague. The symptoms were disgusting: discolored buboes grew in the groin and armpits, making even a light workout next to impossible. And it cut through the population like a deranged hairdresser.

Like **Brexit**, the Black Death split the country in two. One half of them were moaning and despairing, lying on the floor, waiting to die; the other half were getting on with it, facing the challenges, and refusing to talk the country down just because of a plague. Statistically, the only way to protect your partner from the Black Death was to die yourself. Tough choice, unless you were in a truly loveless marriage, like the Prince of Wales was with Lady Diana of the Princess of Wales and the other one in their marriage, whoever it was. Fergie?

It's hard to conceive of a Britain decimated like that: half of everyone dead. Imagine every Christmas watching repeats of the *And Wise Christmas Special*. Imagine The Proclaimer. Imagine Torville. Imagine *Bake Off* without Sue, rather than without Mel and Sue. Imagine the Krankie. Imagine Edward (Jedward without John). Imagine Gregg Wallace on his own in a half empty kitchen with just the forks and none of the knives.

The Black Death really took the shine off the appeal of rats and fleas and shit, and arguably put people off them forever. And if there's one thing to take away from it, it's that, when you have a medieval themed wedding, half the guests should die. And that, even though you got the rest of your life off work if you caught the Black Death (which is a result) the best idea was to avoid it like the plague.

Black Holes

Black Holes are the bits of space that you can't see because they're black. Most of space is quite black, but black holes are really black. Even though nobody can see them because they're black on a black background, scientists know black holes are there because when they ask for money to research them, nobody tells them to fuck off.

Nothing can escape from a black hole, not even David Blaine, which is why they're interesting. We had him trapped for a bit in that glass box, like you might do a spider under a tumbler, but he still got out, so it's important for scientists to work out how to imprison him properly. The answer may be a black hole.

Black holes are infinitely dense, which means they're even tougher than Dime bars. If you tried to eat a black hole, you might break a tooth, which would be disastrous but an interesting story to put on **Facebook**.

Black holes in space may be a gateway to somewhere unexpected that we could hardly imagine. We know this because black holes on Earth, in skirting boards, lead to those weird little mouse houses where they sleep in a matchbox and have a table made of a cotton reel, so it's very likely that black holes elsewhere follow the same rules.

Books

Books are a way of storing information and passing it on to anyone who can read and isn't put off by it being a book. You're holding a book in your hands right now, unless you're not, in which case I'm sorry for making assumptions about the sort of person you are.

In our culture, a book is read from front to back, with the eye traveling along the line of text from the left to the right. The eye then travels back to the left and down to the next line of text. And then from left to right again. And then across to the phone, in case anyone's said anything on Twitter. And then back to the book for a line. Then back to the phone. And down the screen on the phone for about ten minutes. And then back to the book, but back up a line or two to remember where you were and what was happening. Then to the phone again. And so on.

Before phones, books were the only thing people had to read, so they could be a lot bigger. Nowadays big books are only read on long journeys and holidays where the wi-fi coverage is patchy. Some books are good, but they're not about your friends and what they're up to, so they can't be as interesting. And they don't update all the time, so a lot of what happens in books happened ages ago, so it's not as good.

But books still get published, and some even become bestsellers. A really big bestseller may be read by as many people as watch a ten-minute YouTube video about a teenager unboxing mascara brushes, so books are still a very important part of our culture.

The bestselling book of all time is The Bible, by God. Other big books include *50 Shades of Great Expectations* by C. L. Dickings and *The Complete Works of Shakespeare* by **Francis Bacon**. Other important books include Jamie Oliver's *Superfood Family Classics*, *My Story* by Fern Britton, Jamie Oliver's *Food Escapes*, Jamie Oliver's BBQ Book, *Fungus The Bogeyman* and Jamie's *Ministry Of Food*.

Some books were really popular in the past but nobody reads them today, and probably the most famous of these lost classics is the book *The Phone Book*. In the 1960s and 1990s, every home in Britain had a copy of this book, and it's not hard to see why. It wasn't a boring story about a load of made-up people, or even worse only one made-up person, it was this colossal book about literally everybody in the country, with little bits of information about them: exactly what people like to read. You could look up your friends in it or, even better, you could look up yourself, and find out where you lived. In a way, it was the ancestor of the social medias we all look at today on our phones instead of reading books. It updated once a year, like a really slow **Facebook**, and it didn't have pictures, like your phone doesn't when the train goes through a tunnel or into fields. And it was called *The Phone Book* because it was the closest a book came to being as good as a phone in the olden days when nobody had proper phones.

Books are sometimes sold in bookshops, which are shops. Shops are like the real-life version of the internet, but where you can buy less stuff, and you have to leave your house to get there. It's hard to work out why anyone bothers.

························ ✺ ························

Bottles

When we have stuff we put it in a box. But only if it's dry. If it's wet, we put it in a special box called a bottle.

Bottles are tall, thin, see-through boxes with really small lids. You get the wet stuff out of a bottle not by opening the lid, reaching in and taking it out, like you would with dry stuff, but by opening the lid, tipping the bottle and letting the wet stuff out on its own, like it was a pet being let out of a carrier.

We used to know where we were with bottles and boxes. Everyone could agree which was which. And then something new came along: a sinister hybrid, a sort of **Frankingstein**'s storage monster—the carton.

Science can't decide if a carton is a bottle or a box, because it looks like a box but you treat it like a bottle. This sort of identity crisis is everywhere when you start to think about it, which I wish I'd never done. What's a fire extinguisher? Is it a bottle? You can't see into it, like you can with a bottle. Are the ingredients a secret? Or is it like a giant perfume? It sprays like a perfume, so maybe it's a perfume with the superpower of putting out a fire—a sort of superperfume.

The only dry thing you find in bottles is tiny ships. This is probably a sort of a joke about how there should have been water in the bottle. But if it is, I don't get it.

Bowie, David

David Bowie was a series of different singers from between the years 1969 and 2016. Although it was the same person, like **Doctor Who** he regenerated every album or so into a new Bowie.

He was defined by his constantly changing looks. He never went for the obvious, like blacking up or pretending to be a hunchback: he always went for the unexpected, like dressing as the stormy weather symbol off the old weather map, or a big, flat Japanese cock and balls. Whether he was dressed as Herr Flick or a skeleton pirate, or one of your mum's friends from an old Polaroid, he was, in many ways, the Fletch of pop. He had more updates than the Adobe Flash Player.

David Bowie could not only sing, he could also not act, and appeared in several films, playing the homesick alien title character in *E.T.*, and a sort of Duran Duran fairy king in the family film *Muppets Vs The Goblin Crotch*. He even took over Christmas, singing a special carol with Bing Crosby, Stills, Nash and Young, who'd forgotten the words, and being at the start of that cartoon about the snowman sometimes. Although he spoke movingly of his adventures with the snowman, and even showing the scarf he stole off it when it melted, no biography has ever talked about this period of Bowie's life, probably because it was too traumatic a memory.

In 2016, having peaked creatively by meeting Ricky Gervais, David Bowie launched his last persona, the Dead White Dude, and retired from showbusiness.

·························· 🅐 ··························

Brexit

In May 2016, there was this election called a referendum, but it wasn't like normal elections because what you voted for was actually going to happen. But they didn't say that, they kept it as a surprise, which was a nice twist.

Instead of voting for someone you'd never heard of, you got to vote for this place you'd never heard of, called the European Communion. Apparently all the time we thought we'd been the country of Britain, we hadn't been Britain at all, we'd been Europe all along. Like I said, a mad twist. And we hadn't been in charge of ourselves. It was a bit of a shocker. Imagine finding out that the Queen was German or Prince Philip was Greek. It was that crazy. So this was a chance to vote to choose to be Britain again.

There were lots of arguments on both sides, which made it hard to hear what either of them was saying. Some people thought passports were the big issue. With the European passports, you just walked straight through the airport. No queue. That's just not British. We *want* to queue, so getting rid of European passports put us right at the front of the queue to get to the back of a queue, so that's better.

Other people thought that if we left, they'd make spaghetti illegal. And no one wants to have to end up paying a fortune for spaghetti from some dealer in a dodgy flat on a dodgy estate and then getting it home and finding out it was drinking straws or Kerplunk sticks or something.

The leaders of the Remain side were serious people like the prime minister and the chancellor, but the leaders of the Leave side were sort of cartoons, like **Nigel Farridge** and Boris Johnson. And everyone loves a cartoon, so it came as no surprise to anybody that they won.

The United Kingdom had voted for something called a Brexit. Sometimes it's good to vote for something you don't understand, because it means we're all equal. Like it stops you being biased one way or the other. And that's fairer. But almost as soon as the votes were counted, people were asking, "What is a Brexit?" because they realized they didn't know before they said they wanted it. It was a bit like being told to close your eyes and hold out your hands and then being given something you didn't recognize, like a weird thing off a posh menu or Scottish money.

The new prime minister (because the old one had wandered off humming a little tune to himself, like Winnie-The-Pooh) came to the rescue with the answer: "Brexit," she said, "means Brexit." She wasn't wrong. Brexit does mean Brexit. If she wrote that in an exam, you'd have to give her the mark. It's quite clever. I wish I'd done that in mine. "What is 9 x 9?" "9 x 9 = 9 x 9 and you've got to give me the mark. Also, can I be prime minister?"

What was good about Theresa Maybelline's answer was how clear it was. Because sometimes, if you look up a word you don't know in a dictionary, the definition has like loads of words you don't know, and you go from not knowing one word, to not knowing loads, and you feel like a right twat. It reminded me of that old advert: Beanz Meanz Beanz. Or that thing they say about prison: life means life. That means you're going to suffer for ages for making a single stupid decision. And possibly means you're going to die inside. And it's the same with Brexit.

When the UK of GB was in Europe, there was all these words that meant something else. Like "*bonjour*" meant "hello" and "*chapeau*" meant "horse" or "house" or "hat" or something. Now "hat" just means "hat." And Brexit means Brexit. It's simpler. And very hard to argue with. Like a steamroller.

But then, some busybodies started saying that "Brexit means Brexit" wasn't a good enough explanation. So Theresa Maybelline decided to describe it better: Brexit, she said, would be a "red, white and blue Brexit," a reference to our flag, the Union Jacques. What could be more red, white and blue than the British flag? Except perhaps the French flag and the Dutch flag and the Bulgarian flag and the Croatian flag and the Icelandic flag and the Norwegian flag and the Slovakian flag and the Slovenian flag and the Czech flag? It's nice to see what a pan-European Brexit it was going to be, proving how much Britain has in common with its neighbors, if you start with flags. An international brotherhood of Brexit.

The Brexit vote was very close. If it had been just as close but with a different result, the Leave campaign would have demanded a rematch. But the Remain campaign thought it was more polite to remain the losers.

The two sides both had good arguments in the campaign. Look:

What Remain Said

- *We should stay in Europe because leaving is going to devastate the makers of the blue channel at airports. That's jobs that'll probably go overseas now, where blue channels are still allowed.*
- *Everything'll be more expensive now. Except pounds. You'll be able to get them in second hand shops. Or poundshops. Two for a pound.*
- *We should stay in Europe because we get so much good food from there, like omelets and Nutella. We'll have to give that back. And I haven't finished my jar.*
- *If Article 50 is that important, why isn't it Article 1?*

What Leave Said

- *Leave is popular because it's full of happy, rich people like Boris Johnson and Nigel Farridge. And everybody likes happy, rich people.*
- *If the pound goes down in value, you'll get more at Poundstretcher. Like, instead of four Crunchies in a pack, it'll be four Crunchies and a Malteser.*
- *When we leave Europe, we'll be able to go anywhere. Like, we'll be able to move Britain somewhere hotter, like next to Japan or something.*
- *We want immigration under control, so we don't have people like Mark Carney and Madonna and three quarters of Manchester United coming over here.*

You can see why Leave won: a hotter country, with no Madonna, full of happy rich people and cut-price Maltesers.

WHAT HAPPENS NEXT

The exciting answer is it's like a cliffhanger, where they say "To Be Continued…" on the screen, except this time it's a real cliff you're hanging off and not on the telly and there's no words underneath you and this might be the end. But think of that cut-price Malteser.

························· 🜁 ·························

Brush Strokes

Back in the 1980s, TV was in a shocking state. I had a look at an old website about it, and TV back then was this great list of boring stuff nobody remembers now, like *Dallas, The Singing Detective, Cagney & Lacey, Edge Of Darkness, Dynasty, Brideshead*

Revisited, Miami Vice, Boys From The Blackstuff, Fame, Grange Hill, Reilly: Ace Of Spies, Hill Street Blues, The Jewel In The Crown, The Box Of Delights and *That's Life!* which was a documentary about **sausages**, which sounds a lot better than it apparently was.

What was needed was a bloody good laugh. And it came along in September 1986, when *Brush Strokes* first aired on British TV.

Brush Strokes is about a painter, but we never see any of his pictures. Instead we concentrate on his love life, which is much more interesting because no one wants to look at boring pictures. That's why art galleries are always empty, I expect, if they are.

The main character, Jacko, was played by Karl Howman, who was, at the time, medically the most beautiful man ever to appear on television. He had a sidekick called Eric, who looked a bit like Wally from *Where's Wally?* Except you could spot him more easily because he wasn't hidden under a bobble hat.

And if you think the ending of *The Sopranos,* where they all sit in the restaurant and nothing happens, is a big deal, wait until you see the ending of *Brush Strokes.* I won't do spoilers, because it's only been on for about forty years and lots of people haven't seen it (like me, until I YouTubed it just now), but Jacko has to choose between these two women who fancy him, like everyone else (because Jacko is actually made of Karl Howman, who is like a 1980s angel). So Jacko tosses a coin and smiles, but you don't find out which one he chose. Maybe he just decides to spend the coin on chips and that's why he smiles. Everyone likes chips. Anyway, it's an amazing ending, and definitely where *The Sopranos* nicked the idea from. I wonder if they paid Karl Howman for using it.

Cars

Cars are small busses that you can drive yourself. Inside every car is an engine, which is a sort of oven for petrol, but set really high so it always catches fire, like with pizzas. The burning petrol scares the wheels, which try to escape. This makes the car go forwards. To make the car go backward, the car sets fire to the opposite of petrol, which is water. This makes steam, which comes out of the exhaust pipe, as you can see on all cars.

The car was invented in prehistoric times, but because nobody had invented petrol, it worked by putting your feet through the bottom and running while someone played a xylophone really fast and the driver yodeled.

The next sort of car didn't use petrol either—it used a horse at the front, or some butlers in white wigs lifting you up in a chair. When petrol was eventually invented in the 20th century times, all those horses and butlers with wigs were out of work, and had to get jobs as high court judges or supermarket basics lasagnes.

Petrol cars could drive further and faster than butler-powered chairs or even horses, and soon roads had to be built everywhere to cope with demand. Then places to visit were built at the end of the roads, to stop it being a complete waste of time. This was the golden age of motoring, which is what they used to call traffic.

Cars use a lot more of the **environment** than other forms of transport, and also clog up the roads, so the **government** usually tries to make people go on trains instead. Trains use up less resources than other forms of transport because they tend to be cancelled, which is better for the planet. This means people can get on busses instead, and take up space on the roads, which encourages more people to leave their cars at home and get the train, which they can't, because there isn't one.

People get really passionate about cars and go on and on about them. There are car shows, which is hard to imagine, because cars can't dance, unless I've missed something. And there are car rallies, where people park their really shiny cars in a field for everyone to stare at. Cars feature a lot on TV. One of the most popular programs of all time is the program *Top Gear,* but there are also programs about cars, and they are popular too. *Roary the Racing Car* is a good one, as is *DinoTrucks* and *Brum.* It's a shame there isn't a program about cars for grown-ups, because they'd probably be dead into it.

Chaos Theory

Chaos theory is the idea that if a butterfly flaps its wings on one side of the world, there could be a tornado on the other side of the world. It's a neat idea but I'm not sure it's fair to blame butterflies for everything. That's just shifting the blame for all the bad stuff in the world onto something that can't fight back, because it's only made of paper.

After all, by the same logic, a tornado could be caused by anything. Opening a newspaper too fast. Burping. The Queen waving. Any of these things could make a tornado, provided there were enough newspapers or burps or waves. If you're looking for a scapegoat, leave the butterflies alone. Also, it's definitely easier to make the Queen pay for the damage than it is to ask a butterfly to cough up. She's minted. And that way you're making a practical contribution to fixing the problem, rather than just having a go at insects.

·· ∫ ··

Children's Television

Television comes in three types: stuff for normal people, like *Storage Wars* and *Bargain Hunt;* stuff for old people, like *Rip-Off Britain* and *Can't Pay? We'll Take It Away;* and stuff for kids. Kids' TV (or "Children's Television," to give it its medical term) is usually shorter, more colorful and shitloads better than everything else on TV. Plus, it's a hotbed of radical politics and progressive issues, shaping the minds of tomorrow with animal antics and stuff that looks like it belongs in one of them wonky dreams you have when you've got flu.

ADVENTURE TIME

A boy and his animal struggle with the realities of everyday life. *Kes,* basically.

THE AMAZING WORLD OF GUMBALL

Absolutely brilliant series about inclusivity. A cat called Gumball has a best friend who's a fish, showing kids that they can live in harmony with their enemies. Presumably based on the teachings of Christ, which would explain why the enemy is called Darwin. At last count, there are about a million episodes.

BAGPUSS

A disabled cat who's in charge of a sort of filthy junk shop over-run with mice.

BOD

An absolutely revolutionary cartoon, the likes of which we still haven't seen today.

It was set in a futuristic place where there was hardly any things, and not even a horizon, and sometimes not even the ground. It starred Bod, who was the first gender non-binary cartoon character, long before this became socially accepted. Bod shared his or her world with his or her aunt, a postman, a farmer, a policeman and an off-screen piccolo player. It was, like George Orwell's *Down On The Farm,* a story about one thing which is actually about another thing: the Soviet Union.

The policeman represents the state. The farmer represents the worker. The postman represents the secret service. Aunt Flo represents someone called the proletariat. Bod represents the dutiful citizen. And the piccolo player represents the dreams of a bright Communist future. At least, that's what this essay by a film school student on radicalcartooninterpretations.com says.

Still, the music was good, because it was short.

FIREMAN SAM

A show about how accident-prone the Welsh are.

GRANGE HILL

Bleak, gritty series meant to make kids unhappy, like greens or exams or the dentist. And a sort of breeding-ground for *EastEnders* actors.

IN THE NIGHT GARDEN

A freezing cold punk goes to sleep on a tiny boat that's obviously lost at sea. The stars shine in the night sky and turn into flowers. The flowers are actually blossom on a tree in a big garden with a bandstand in the middle of it and a fucking great hedge all the way around it so people can't see what goes on in there. Understand it yet? Neither do I.

The punk's got a girlfriend called Whoopsy or something, and a friend who's a sort of WALL·E made of cushions who collects stones as if that's a rational thing for a robot sofa to do. There's a sort of Sugababes tribute act called the Wombliboos, and one of them tourist trains you see at the seaside, except it's obviously being driven by a deranged maniac, and two Amish families that live in a tree trunk.

Everyone in the show has had so much plastic surgery that their faces hardly move, which I'm not sure sets a good example to young girls. But, then, I'm not its audience and maybe kids these days are more relaxed about trout pouts and designer vaginas.

OCTONAUTS

A white-knuckle adventure series, like a sort of underwater *A-Team,* made up of three animals you always find living in the sea: a cat, a polar bear and a penguin who is a qualified doctor. They have special vehicles like all heroes do, except for Nelson Mandela who just had a nice family saloon. He didn't even have an ice cream van, like the Pope does. I suppose that's what makes him a hero: battling against adversity (not having an ice-cream van) to achieve great things (whatever it is he did).

PEPPA PIG

A family of giggling pigs live on a hill in a parallel universe where NO ONE EVER MENTIONS **SAUSAGES**. They snort like pigs but talk like humans except they NEVER MENTION **SAUSAGES**. The show is banned in China, so it must be sending out secret messages. Though, obviously, NOT ONES ABOUT **SAUSAGES**.

THE SIMPSONS

A heartwarming show about a nice little ordinary American town where everyone has jaundice. It's based on a true story. You can tell this because **Donald Trump** gets made president in one episode, although that was before he was president so it's based on true events that haven't happened yet, which is the closest human beings have ever come to time travel. It's no wonder kids love it. They always want to know what happens next. They're rubbish with surprises.

China

China is the busiest country on Earth. This is because it's got the most people and because literally everything is made there, apart from cheese. Cheese is made in France if it's soft, Britain if it's hard and Italy if it's a sort of yellow metal.

The Chinese make everything because they invented everything. They're the cleverest people in the world. They invented paper, gunpowder, the compass, steel, printing—and sweet and sour sauce.

Sweet and sour sauce is the most amazing of all the sauces after ketchup. And even ketchup is basically cold sweet and sour sauce. When you order Chinese food, there's always a variety of sauces, but they're all sweet and sour with different names. Satay is sweet and sour with peanuts. Kung Po is sweet and sour with chili and garlic. Sichuan is sweet and sour with soy sauce. Curry sauce is curry. I don't think that one's from China, so you can only have it on chips.

What's so clever about sweet and sour sauce is the combination of sweet and sour, which are almost opposites. Who'd have thought that combining sweetness—the essence of toffee and marshmallow and Bailey's—with sourness—the essence of lemon and gooseberry and pickles—would produce something that wasn't as utterly sickening as pickled marshmallow or lemon Bailey's? And yet, because they're so clever, the Chinese pulled it off.

Now, sweet and sour sauce is the Chinese national dish—it's their version of the British national dish, the Meal Deal (sandwich, fizz, crisps, bar). There are probably sweet and sour sauce machines on every street corner in China. I don't know. I haven't been there. I don't want to. It looks full.

In fact, thanks to the ingenuity of the Chinese, we can combine many of their inventions into what must be the most Chinese possible thing to do: read a menu printed (invented in China) on paper (invented in China) and order a sweet and sour dish (invented in China) from a takeaway (almost certainly invented in China) using an **iPhone** (assembled in China) which will be delivered by a man on a steel (invented in China) motorbike with an L-plate on the back, finding your home using a compass (invented in China) on his way to a fireworks display (invented in China) while you eat your sweet and sour chicken off a plate (made of China).

Also, there's noodles.

•••••••••••••••••••••••••••••• ♪ ••••••••••••••••••••••••••••••

Clapping

For many years, the only sounds that came out of human beings came out of their bums or their mouths. Then, one day in once upon a time, primitive man discovered he had noise in his hands.

These days, clapping is taken for granted, like shoes and doors. And we clap for all sorts of reasons: we clap to applaud a performance; we clap to get attention; and, of course, everyone claps in the shower.

Since clapping was discovered, new forms of hand noise have been coming thick and fast: there's clicking the fingers, there's doing that rapper's snap thing and there's hand farting, which everyone goes through a phase of. There's also high-fiving, which is sort of social clapping—when you high-five, instead of clapping with both your own hands, you clap one of your hands with one of someone else's—that way, no one can claim the noise is theirs alone. This is particularly good for people whose hands, through no fault of their own, make no noise at all. Tragically, some people are afflicted by this, and silent hands is still something there is no cure for.

Musicians are snobs about clapping, and insist that you never clap on the dot of one o'clock and three o'clock, but always on two and four. This is why you should never have lunch with a musician. That and they've never got their half of the bill.

.... ♪ ....

Climate Change

Our planet is changing, and not in a good way, like into a butterfly or a giant magic shoe. It's changing into something called a climate change. And we're all to blame.

Climate change doesn't just change the climate, it also changes its name. All the time. It used to be global warming. Before that it was the Oz One layer, then acid rain, and when I was small, it was just called the **weather** forecast. Which is why it's so hard for humans to make it stop. Because nobody knows its name, and it doesn't care. Like a tortoise. Or a boat.

Climate change is a big challenge for all of us. Like when it looks like it's going to rain, and you put on a big coat, and then it's really hot and you have to spend all day carrying your coat and sitting on it. But for the whole planet.

Climate change has always been with us, except in the olden days, it was natural, not man made. A bit like socks. Nineteen centuries ago, there was an **Industrial Revolution**, which meant everything worked off coals. Coals is a fossil fuel, which is basically setting fire to dinosaurs. All the **gas** inside dinosaurs comes out when you burn them and stays in the sky. And it's this dirty dead dinosaur gas that's to blame for climate change. And so many **dinosaurs** were burned for steam trains that nowadays there is almost no dinosaurs left, except the ones in the middle of the Earth, and a few in Jurassic Parks.

Rising temperatures are a worldwide problem. I'm dictating this into my phone and it's eleven degrees outside. But if scientists are right, in fifty years' time, today will be thirteen degrees. Although I'll have a better phone.

Our Industrial Revolution is finished, but now China wants one. Which is selfish of them. And that's why people are worried, because China's climate change could blow anywhere, thanks to wind farms. As the Earth heats up, both of the North Poles melt, and the sea goes up. Which is bad news for anybody who doesn't want to live in a sea. Like humans. Or the Little Mermaid. She hated it. Wouldn't stop going on about it.

Every one of us is responsible for climate change, and people in the olden days too. The **government** says we need to cut our greenhouse gas emissions by 2050. But if, like me, you don't have a greenhouse, they say you can still reduce something called your carbon footprint by not flying and walking more. But my feet swell up when I walk, which is why I go to Ibiza in a plane. Because the last thing the planet needs is my big, swollen footprint, carboning everywhere.

What can we do about climate change?

There are simple things we can all do. We should all try and use less climate. So when it rains, go inside. Make sure there's some for everyone. Buckets can be used to catch rain, and solar panels can catch sunshine, and then that weather can be flown quickly round the world, to where it's needed. Something as simple as that can make a big difference.

Climate change is directly linked to how much energy we use. Because the more we leave things on, the hotter they get. Even proper lightbulbs get hot. Something as simple as leaving your lights on could affect the ice at the North Poles. Look at your fridge. The light goes off when you close the door. And the fridge is full of ice. Which just goes to show.

Global warming doesn't just mean more hot days: it also means more cold days. And more of both sorts of day must mean the year is getting longer. So by the time I'm fifty, I'll be seventy. And that's serious. Because old people stay indoors more with the radiators on, and that's global warming sped up right there.

But not everyone thinks climate change is real. This hot topic has split the science community right down the middle, 90/10. Some scientists, like Jeremy Clarkson and **Donald Trump,** say fossil fuels are the only way to keep the economy going, so we should use them all up as quickly as possible. But if they're wrong and climate change is happening, we face the nightmare scenario that our grandchildren may never see a rainbow. Except in a zoo.

There's a difference between thinking climate change is man made, and thinking climate change is made up. But I can't remember it. Because I'm too hot. And that might be a warning to us all. A global warning.

Color

Color is the reflection or absorption of light or something on the something length or something. That's the science bit. But for most people, color is a way of understanding the world. Whether it's traffic lights, clothes or crisp flavors (but mostly crisp flavors), colors are our guides to whether we should stop or go, show which team we're on, or choose cheese and onion over salt and vinegar (cheese and onion).

In olden times, there was only seven colors, one for each day of the week. We know this, because of the rainbow. The first rainbow appeared on p.26 of the Bible, when God put it there as a sort of "sorry about that, mate" gift for Noah to make up for the colossal flood he'd chucked all over the poor man's zoo boat.

There's been a lot of debate about which color is which day. We know the order of the rainbow: Red Orange Yellow Green Battle In Vain. But it's obvious that Red is the best day, so that can't be Monday. Either it's Friday (which is drinks) or it's Saturday (which is a lie-in). It can't be Sunday, because *Antiques Roadshow* is on, and that means the end of fun, and that it's time to get all serious and sad again about going back to work tomorrow.

In 1958, boffins at crayon company Crayola discovered a whole load more colors, including Brown, Lavender, Goldenrod, Maroon, Turquoise and Silver. Suddenly it was possible to draw things like trees and lavender, something which just hadn't been possible until then unless you did them in silhouette.

Which brings us to the difficult subject of black and white.

Black and white, which are obviously colors, aren't. They're sort of anti-colors. We know they've been around for hundreds of years, because of pianos. But we don't know how they got in or why they got banned from the rainbow. We know they were mortal enemies for many years, and probably battled it out again and again (remembered today in chess), but what they fell out over is lost to the mists of time. Mists which are gray, just like black and white both are.

Some colors are shorthand for things. Red typically means danger, which is why busses and lions are red. Blue is associated with water, which is why school uniforms and the Co-Op is blue. And yellow is associated with the glory of nature, which is why bulldozers and Primula are yellow.

Some people are color-blind, which means they can't see color—so everything to them looks old-fashioned, which must be amazing, because imagine getting a Nintendo Switch and it looking old-fashioned. You'd feel like a robot from the future.

Computers

Computers are all around us. In offices, computer shops and computer repair shops. It's hard to think of anything that doesn't have a computer in it, except cows. And they've probably got computers in them now.

Computers have become part of our culture. People staring into their phones instead of looking where they're going have become commonplace. But you have to ask the question: Are we looking at the computers or are the computers looking at us? And even though the answer to that question is obvious, it sounds spooky.

The computer was invented by Charles Babbage in 1822, but it didn't have a screen so no one knew what it was doing. Then Konrad Zooooooze managed to invent a proper computer in Germany in 1936, but that one got bombed up by the British. And that meant we in Britain could invent it first again, thanks to a man named by the name of Alan Turing, at Bletchley Parks, in War Two.

Unlike today's computers, those early computers were made of transistors and paper and pipes. And they were absolutely huge. They didn't have mouses, but if they did, they'd have been the size of **cars** and you'd have had to sit in your mouse like a little bumper car, and drive them about to make YouTube work. And each YouTube video would have been the size of a car park, and if you were watching porn, someone over the road would have easily been able to see, so it's no wonder they had to make do with What The Butler Saw machines and Linda Lusardi, and Britain never really became a first-class porn-watching nation until the 21st Minnellium century.

The invention of the computer was a primary benefit to one particular group of people: video game players. Until computers, you could only play Super Mario using a pen and paper or colored bits of dough. And a game of Pac-Man could take three days to set up, if the peas kept rolling off the table. The computer changed all that.

Before computers, if you wanted to send an email, you had to print it out and put it in an envelope. And if you wanted to pretend to steal a car or beat up a prostitute, you couldn't just power up Grand Theft Auto, you had to be in *The Bill*.

Now, there's almost nothing a person can do that a computer can't, except ride a horse. So lots of jobs have been replaced by computers. Perhaps one day we'll have a computer Queen, with the real Queen just used for the bits that are on a horse.

Even as sophisticated as they now are, computers are still basically machines for doing fast sums. Like, if you're trying to add up while being chased by a shark, you need a computer. Inside a computer are lots of ones and noughts. Computers use ones and noughts because you can fit more of those in a small space, because they're the smallest numbers. And computers keep getting smaller. The time can't be far off where you'll be able to get one the size of a phone. Or even smaller than that, like the size of an old phone.

Computers can think even quicker than humans. Like, I've just thought about crisps—but a computer could think about crisps even before I'd written "I've just thought about." It's scary to think that one day, we won't need to think about crisps at all, and maybe that will be the day we surrender to the robots once and for all.

Alan Turing, the weird man who discovered computers, is now a national hero, and people queue for ages to touch the Turing Shroud. There are even computers made of cloud now. What next? A computer you can eat? Or fight? Computer music? Who knows? Maybe a computer does. Of, if it doesn't know, it will one day. That's the magic of computers.

························· ✍ ·························

Corbyn, Jeremy

There used to be this program on called *The Amazing Adventures Of Morph,* about this brown naked man and his white naked friend who lived in a box along with a brush and some tin foil in the shape of a girl. It was sort of an example of interracial harmony among the Plasticine community. And there was this other character in it called Grandmorph, a sort of muttering, tetchy old man, who might have been an Orkney crofter or a divorced librarian or something but was very much a side character who most people would struggle to imagine as the center of the story.

Jeremy Corbyn is the leader of the Labour Party.

Crime

One in twenty people have been a victim of crime. That means that nineteen out of twenty people are criminals, which is a terrifying statistic. It's no wonder we need police.

In the olden days, before the police was discovered, if someone did something wrong, there was nothing you could do except write to Robin Hood or form a mob with your neighbors and hunt them down and kill them, like they still do in bits of Croydon. But today, we've got one other option, thanks to Sir Robert Peel who, in 1829, discovered the police.

Once the police had been discovered, victims of crime knew who to ask for help, because of their special hats, designed to be visible at a distance by people being murdered in the London fog.

Police try to stop crime—but couldn't exist without it. If there was no crime, what would they do all day, except putting addresses on bikes with that hammer? If no one's going to steal those bikes, that's just decorating, and much harder to justify as a reasonable spending of taxpayers' money.

Of course, there's no point fighting crime if you don't know what crime is. That's why rules come in: rules called laws.

The first laws was the Ten Commandments, which was left on a hill by God. And most of them—killing, gravity and the one about not interfering with oxes—are still used today, even though God is dead. That's because they were carved in stone, and can never be forgotten, just like whatever it was Ed Miliband wrote on that slab.

But other laws have changed. Taking it up the bum used to be against the law, but now you're a bit of a fridge if you don't at least one week a month. Who knows, one day the same might be true of burglary or racism.

These days there are laws for everything. Apparently it's illegal to steal music or clothes, even if you walk out of Topshop wearing them because you sort of forgot you were trying them on.

They say the punishment should fit the crime. But what if you've stolen a train? They'd need to steal a train from you in return, and surely if you had a train, you wouldn't have stolen a train in the first place. Otherwise they're just taking their train back. And you go free. That doesn't feel right.

When society decides that something is wrong, like stealing or murder, and you disagree with society, you get put in prison, with a load of people who agree with you. So everybody's happy.

Think about it: if there wasn't police, we'd be able to do what we liked, which is great. But police wouldn't be able to do what they liked, which is be the police. And that would be against their human rights.

.... 🎷 ....

Cunk, Philomena

It doesn't matter how much so-called information you know, if you don't know yourself. So I have filled in a questionnaire. This won't help you understand yourself, because it's me, but it did help me, so maybe it will help you, particularly if you ignore my answers and imagine your own instead. It really is that simple. I don't know why Buddhists make such a bloody fuss about it.

FIRST NAME? Cunk
LAST NAME? Philomena
BIRTHDAY? Yes. Every year
HEIGHT? 5m 10cm

WEIGHT? 5'10"

STAR SIGN? Aspel

FAVORITE MEAL? Jelly and **ice cream**

WHEN WERE YOU HAPPIEST? Just then. Thinking about jelly and ice cream.

IF YOU COULD LIVE ANYWHERE IN THE WORLD, WHERE WOULD YOU LIVE? Stevenage or a volcano

WHAT DID YOU WANT TO BE WHEN YOU GREW UP? Emlyn Hughes

WHAT IS YOUR FAVORITE DESTINATION? Upstairs

WHAT ONE ITEM WOULD YOU SAVE IF YOUR HOUSE WAS ON FIRE? My house

WHAT IS THE LAST FILM YOU SAW? *Nutty Professor II: The Klumps*

FAVORITE FILM OF ALL TIME? *Nutty Professor II: The Klumps*

CAN YOU SPEAK ANOTHER LANGUAGE? Why?

WHEN WAS THE LAST TIME YOU CRIED? *Nutty Professor II: The Klumps*

DO YOU SHARE YOUR HOME WITH ANY ANIMALS? Roast chicken and spiders

WHAT ONE SONG MEANS THE MOST TO YOU? Elton John by The Lion King

WHO WOULD BE YOUR DREAM DINNER PARTY GUESTS, LIVING OR DEAD? Carol Vorderman and the Abominable Snowman. Also someone who can cook (maybe one of the Hairy Bikers) and someone who understands cutlery (not a Hairy Biker. They look like they eat with their feet.)

WHEN AND WHERE WAS YOUR FIRST KISS? 1986. Armpit.

.... 𝄞 ....

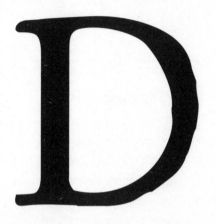

Dark Ages, The

The Dark Ages are an era we don't understand, with very little of it recorded. They were very much the BBC4 of their day.

Hardly anything is known about the Dark Ages. We don't even know if they were dark, or if they lasted ages. They're a mystery to us, which is why it's odd their name doesn't reflect that. They were like a sort of historical Airbnb where no one has written in the visitors' book, or a place on TripAdvisor with no reviews. Anything could have happened in the Dark Ages, but probably didn't, or we'd have heard about it.

·· 🗑 ··

Democracy

All of nature (apart from maybe daisies and waterfalls) is a brutal struggle for power. Animals and monsters fight to decide who's in charge. But unlike animals and monsters, people don't have to fight for power: instead, we do a vote—a vote that would be as much of a waste of time as, say, standing about in a primary school you don't even go to, if it wasn't for something called democracy.

Britain is often called the oldest democracy in the world, because we've had about twenty whole elections that everyone could vote in, going back almost a hundred years. It's hard to think back that far, so associated is the land of **Shakespeare** and Stonehenge and **Henry of Eight** with that long, proud century of democracy. It's easy to imagine a country without modern conveniences like the steam train and the computer, but not without British democracy.

But, if the Keystage 2 history revision Bitesize quiz page is to be believed, democracy dates back even more back than that. It was invented in Greece, like thick yogurt, sodomy and **triangles**, by the Romans. The word "democracy" comes from the Greek word "democratic," which means it's been around ages.

Democracy probably came to Britain on rats, which is the usual way things are spread in olden times. Maybe they'd eaten some. Rats eat anything.

But what is democracy?

Democracy means that it doesn't matter who you are, your vote matters exactly the same: not very much.

Modern non-Greek democracy began 800 years ago, in knights-in-armor times, at Runnymede (which sounds worse than it is). Britain used to be ruled by a king or queen, just like now—except, back then, they were treated like a god, rather than a slightly better-off version of someone off *Made In Chelsea*. When you look at it, royal behavior was a total shithouse, until eventually the people rose up and made King John sign something called Magma Carta.

According to Google Translate, "Magma Carta" is Latin for "cardboard volcano." Nobody knows why, but it shook up Britain just like a cardboard volcano would, if one erupted in Leicester, showering everyone in corrugated rocks and devastating the region with a barrage of papercuts that would leave emergency services struggling.

Magma Carta itself was less a cardboard volcano and more a sort of menu, telling people what rights and lefts were available. It was signed under a yew tree. Yew tree didn't mean then what it does now. Then it was just a tree, rather than a systematic round-up of radio perverts.

Soon Britain had its own parliament, which could stop the king doing what he wanted, by a simple, formal process of cutting his head off. But by 1605, parliament had become so annoying that it was nearly blown up by Guy Forks, inventor of the fork. But the British Parliament survived, in one of the world's most iconic buildings—the home of democracy: Hogwarts.

In the UK, people vote for people to represent people, like mascots. Each of these mascots is called an MP, which stands for parliament. There are 100 MPs in an MPound. In the olden days, only men could vote, but one day a lady called Sufferer Jet was run over by a king on a horse, and to make up for this, women got the vote, and could at last decide which man should be in charge. Since women got the vote, there have been eleven Labour governments, ten Conservative governments and two collision governments. Now, everyone in Britain can vote, unless they're under eighteen, in prison, or lost.

Someone who didn't agree with democracy was Adolf Hitler. He tried to invade Britain and take it over as a dictator, though mainly he wanted his ball back, which double agents posted in the nation's music halls had informed him was in the Albert Hall. It's not clear how his ball had ended up there—maybe he'd hit it too hard during a game of golf. Luckily Hitler never managed to get to Britain and died, still playing golf, in a bunker.

Britain is a proper democracy, yet a third of the population still can't be arsed to vote, so instead, they exercise their democratic right to moan. Moaning is a bit like voting, except you don't have to go to a primary school and stand in a cupboard to moan. You can do it wherever you want. Which makes it more convenient for people with bad feet or a dog.

Democracy is a bit like a Harvester: you can choose whatever you want. Or you can just have nothing. That's the beauty of democracy: you don't have to have loads of salad to cover up the fact you've got five sausages in your bowl. You don't have to stand up and be counted. You can sit down and be ignored if you like, because that's your democratic right: you can choose not to matter. And that matters. If you want it to. It's up to you.

Why the X?

Nobody knows why we put a cross in the box on the ballot paper instead of a tick. Perhaps it's because a cross has two lines so takes longer to draw than a tick that only has one and a half lines. That means you have a bit more time to think over the important decision of who is going to be the most powerful person in your country.

Digestion

The human body, like any animal, needs a source of food to function. And the source of food that the human body uses as a

source of food is food. Food is broken down into a form the body can use in a process called digestion which is the scientific term for "lunch."

Digestion starts in the mouth, which is a sort of tunnel in your face. If you didn't have a mouth, the rest of the digestive system would have trouble getting to the food, which would be on a plate, much too far away for even the strongest stomach to reach. In a way, you could say that digestion starts with the hands, because they hold the knife and fork, but I've been out with people who eat by just putting their faces straight into their dinner. I say "people," but I did that only once, because I take that sort of behavior as a warning—still, science has to take those monsters into account.

In the mouth, food is chewed up with teeth (or, in the case of jelly, swooshed through them) and mixed with spit. It's funny that if someone mixed your food with bodily fluids before serving it to you in a restaurant, it would be seen as a grave insult (or normal if you were Michael Winner) and lose them at least one star on their TripAdvisor rating, but your food won't work at all unless you splosh it about with a load of gob.

The spat-on food then passes to the ostrophagus, named after the ostrich, because of how they are always getting coconuts stuck in their necks, like you see in cartoons. The ostrophagus is a pipe that goes all the way down to your stomach, muscles pushing it all the way. It would be a lot less tiring if the pipe was shorter and your stomach was in, say, your shoulders. But luckily we get lots of energy from food which we can use to power the muscles that are needed to eat the food that powers our muscles that eat the food that we use to power the muscles that eat our food.

There are loads of pipes in our bodies, and not all of them are for food. Some are for blood, some are for breathing and some are for broadband. When we swallow our food, a flap blocks our windpipe to stop the food going down the wrong pipe into our lungs, where it would be less useful. Nobody wants that. Imagine a balloon full of vegetable soup, and how

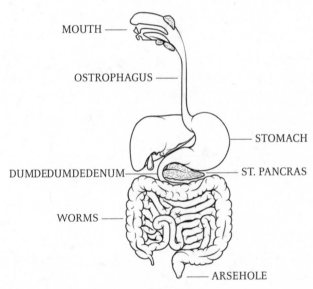

MOUTH ——

OSTROPHAGUS ——

—— STOMACH

DUMDEDUMDEDENUM—— —— ST. PANCRAS

WORMS ——

—— ARSEHOLE

The Digestive System

upset you'd be if you got one of those when you finished all your **ice cream** at Giraffe.

After the stomach, the food then goes somewhere else. It gets a bit squashed up in the diagram and it's hard to see what's what. It's a kind of full English breakfast thing. There's a bit that looks like fat worms, and some cushion things that seem important. They've got labels on, but I can't quite see where the lines are pointing. There's a liver, and a St. Pancras, and a dumdedumdede-num and the food goes through all of them doing something or other. Finally, the food we have eaten simply disappears, having done all it needs to. Nobody knows where it goes.

At the bottom of the digestive system is the best bit, the bottom, or as scientists call it, "the arsehole." This is the bit round the corner where (milk milk lemonade etc.) chocolate's made. Nobody knows where the chocolate comes from. It is one of the many mysteries of the human body, that it can produce so much disgusting stuff for no good reason.

Dinosaurs

In the really olden days, long before even the olden days, the only people on Earth was dinosaurs. Dinosaurs were sort of giant roaring monsters, like that huge bloke in *The Princess Bride.*

There are loads of sorts of dinosaurs, but the main ones are the across ones and the up and down ones. The across ones ate grass, and the up and down ones ate the across ones. It was just like lions and whatever those stripey piano-horses are that lions eat.

Across

Up and Down

Dinosaurs ruled for ages and ages, very much like our own queen, until they were replaced by shy, less interesting mouse-like creatures who spent most of their time hiding amongst plants, like our own Prince Charles.

Something killed the dinosaurs. We don't know what. Some experts think they died because they crawled under the ground, into rocks, making it hard for them to breathe. Monsters like that are too stupid to live. Whatever it was that killed the dinosaurs, it turned them all to stone, like some horrible creature from a film. We can only hope whatever did it never comes back.

Some scientists say that dinosaurs revolved into birds. But dinosaurs are much too heavy to fly, because they're made of stone. So that's just one of those crazy theories to file with the Earth being flat, and the Earth being round.

You don't need to go to Jurassic Park in America to see dinosaurs these days. Like most things, we've got our own in Britain, but not as good. In London, there's a Victorian zoo called the National History Exhibition that still has dinosaurs. But when you see the appalling conditions they are kept in—starving, just bones, really—it's surprising there are any left at all. The sad story of the abuse of one such dinosaur by a vicious Victorian is famously told in the film *The Elephant Man.*

Doctor Who

Doctor Who is a television program about this eccentric man who worked for the BBC in the 60s and 70s.

The man, who is dressed in weird clothes, persuades teenagers to get into a cupboard with him by offering them Jelly Babies and fixing it for them to go on dream trips and meet famous and important people. He takes them away from their families and the kids are in great danger while they're with him, so there's a lot of screaming. Everything he does is aimed at children, but it's a bit peculiar, because kids get really scared, and the things they see him do are seared into their memories, so they grow up a bit odd and can't really think about anything else.

It's a total fantasy and very far fetched, which is part of the fun, because it's a bit frightening, so it's good it could never happen.

.... 🗑 ....

Domesday Book, The

In 1086 a book was published which was the *Fifty Shades Of Its Day* of its day. Except it had a more ominous name that made it sound like a survival manual for when the **zombies** take over.

The Domesday Book isn't as gloomy as that, although it must have sounded it. "It's fine, nothing to worry about—it's just called the Domesday Book. I just need to know everything about you..." Because that's what it is: a very old and very long list of everybody in the country, where they lived and what stuff they had. It was medieval **Facebook**. It knew everything about everybody, and it was written by everybody about everything.

King William I, who commissioned it, was a sort of Marcus Zuckerberg The Elder. But unlike today's Mark Zuckerberg, he was actually interested in tax. That's why he asked for the Domesday Book—although he didn't need a reason. There's no point being king unless you can ask for stupid shit.

Unlike Facebook, you couldn't click on the Domesday Book,

and it was no good trying to use it to get off on your exes. "Seven cottages and three men's plow teams" is a tough wank. Although, to be fair, it's a start.

There were two main jobs listed in the Domesday Book: peasant and peasant counter. Peasants lived in thatched wooden huts full of chicken shit. The water was filthy, so everyone drank beer, and the only thing to eat was bread. It must have been a particularly challenging time for the gluten intolerant; but luckily nobody was middle class yet, so they just put up with it.

And this Great British Stock Take recorded everything: fields, sheep, worms, even clouds. It was like Google Street View, in that it was probably out of date by the time they finished it. Still, the unique technology of the Domesday Book was single-handedly responsible for dragging Britain kicking and screaming into the **Middle Ages**.

The Domesday Book is still in print today, which is mad because it's borderline unreadable and literally no one has ever finished it. It was very much the internet of its day.

Dressage

Horses dancing. Well weird. They should do more sports like this. There should be a sport where cows write novels, or one where they see which donkeys can make the best cakes. I wonder if horses dance like this when people aren't on them. You'd have to go to a horse disco to find out, and I've no idea where those are. They probably flyer them quite specifically to other dancing horses, in case the police horses come and close them down.

Dyer, Danny

Danny Dyer is probably the greatest actor of his generation.

Born Danial Dandy Dan D. Dyer on his birthday in 1977, he rose to fame. His first big film appearance was as one half of the title role in *Human Traffic*. But he is probably best known for his tear-breaking performance as landlord Mick Carter in the never-ending TV drama *EastEnders*.

Dyer brings his tremendous sensitivity and range to his work. In the epic romantic film *Run For Your Wife*, he brings everything you'd expect to the character of John Smith. And when he appeared as Danny Dyer in *Who Do You Think You Are?*, critics praised the moving scenes in which he discovered that he had ancestors.

He is also known as a fiercely outspoken commentator, and has famously suggested that cocaine is an excellent reward for a job well done, that cutting your ex's face is a good way of getting over her and that breaking Mark Kermode's nose is a good way of getting over him.

He should definitely be the next James Bond.

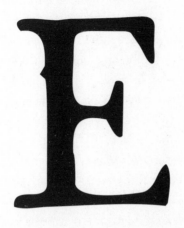

Electricity

Electricity is a way of making things light up, or come on, or move, or stand on end. The simplest way to understand electricity is to rub a balloon on your jumper. If you put the balloon on your head, your **hair** stands on end. That's electricity.

In power stations, because balloons are expensive, they use **atoms**, which are like little balloons, when you look up close. Because they're smaller, they're cheaper and you can have more of them, so there's more electricity.

Without electricity, your hair would just stay on your head all the time, getting bored. If enough electricity gets together in one place, it turns into a lightbulb and can be put to use. Otherwise it's mainly for moving hair. You can tell this because if you put your finger in a plug socket, the first thing that happens is your hair goes up on end, before you explode. Frankly, it's one of those experiments that's probably better to hear about than to do.

Electricity is measured in Volts, Amps and Watts. Volts are how many electricities there are; Amps are how fast they're going and Watts is how much you care.

The word electricity comes from the word "electric," meaning "to do with electricity," and "city," meaning "a place where there's a lot of electricity." To get electricity to where it's needed, there are wires. Wires are like metal hair, and to stop all the wires standing on end, which would be useless, they're kept in the walls of your house, or stuck to big pylons in the countryside. (Pylons are like big electrees.)

Of course, any scientist will tell you, there's more to electricity than balloons and hair standing on end. Other uses of electricity include those glass balloon things with lightning in them that make your hair stand on end—and hairdryers, which use electricity to dry your hair by blowing it, like air coming out of a balloon, and make your hair stand on end.

There is a dark side to electricity though, because balloons are bad for the **environment** because they strangle puffins and get caught inside tortoises. It is possible to generate electricity in a more natural way. Wind turbines can be used to make people's hair stand on end without needing a balloon, and maybe they are the future of electricity. One day we may have electric **cars** and even electric televisions, thanks to the hair-moving power of wind.

End of the World, The

Some things feel like they're going to go on forever: love, life, the film *Eyes Wide Shut*—but nothing does. Everything comes to an end. And the world will come to an end one day.

A million years ago, a scientist called Nostradamus predicted the world would come to an end in a huge mess called a pocalypse. The word "pocalypse" is just posh dictionary code for "the end of days," which is just sunset, which happens all the time, which is why the world didn't end just like Nostradamus said it would.

But Nostradamus wasn't the only one who reckoned the pocalypse was coming. As well as inventing Minecraft, the ancient Mayan civilization predicted that the world as we knew it would end in 2012. Luckily, it turned out just to be Ceefax that ended that year. And that was only the whole world if you were over sixty and housebound.

In Victoria times, another pocalypse was predicted by Mother Shipton, a mystic from Yorkshire who lived in a cave because at the time that was better than living in Yorkshire, just like it also is now. She wrote, "The world to an end will come, in eighteen hundred and eighty one," a claim which has recently been debunked by experts, through a careful process of looking around and seeing the world is still here.

Predicting the end of the world is tricky, and you're best leaving it to the experts. Probably the biggest experts are the Jehovah's Witnesses, who have predicted the end of the world in 1914, 1915, 1918, 1920, 1925, 1941, 1975, 1994 and 1997, so are getting really good at it. It is interesting to notice that they didn't predict any ends of the world between 1986 and 1991, which is when the BBC ran the painting and decorating sitcom *Brush Strokes*.

The most famous pocalypse of all is in bestselling historical thriller *The Bible*. Like the film *Seven*, *The Bible* ends with a sort of mass killing based on the number seven. A lamb with seven horns and seven eyes opens seven seals. The first one contains the four horsemen of the pocalypse. You wouldn't think seals would eat horses, but pocalypses are full of nasty surprises. The second seal contains a red horse, the third seal contains a black horse and the fourth seal contains a pale horse, so it turns out horses are actually seals' favorite food.

The seventh seal contains seven trumpets, and when they start tooting, the Earth catches fire and things start falling out of the sky: not normal things like snowflakes or birdshit, but huge things like a mountain and a star. And on and on it goes, with more seven more things and seven more seven more things. It's more baffling than *Golden Balls*. It's like *Deal Or No Deal?* where each of the boxes contains deformed farmyard animals. Really scary ones with wrong eyes. Creatures even more terrifying than the original Bungle.

Perhaps the writers of *The Bible* were confusing the end of the world with the end of *The Bible*, because that's how *The Bible* ends.

To know how the world will really end, we have to turn to science. And science says it won't be a giant destructive seven times table after all. It could be Artificial Intelligence—which is when the Speak & Spells and Gameboys and Bluetooth speakers rise up and take over the Earth—or man-made **climate change** (unless we decide to only use natural climates)—or a nasteroid giving us a good clout—or a supervolcano. There's a supervolcano hiding under America, apparently. Let's hope nobody finds it or there'll be hell to pay.

There have been times when it's felt like the end of the world, but, at least so far, we haven't had the pocalypse. By the time this book comes out, though, that may all have changed, and you might be reading this from a fiery pit of shattered glass, eating each other's scabs and fighting for the benefit of a radioactive Tina Turner. If so, maybe all I can say is: take care—and take one last look at our beautiful world.

Environment, The

The environment is everything around us, but not the interesting bits. It includes the sky, mud, rainbows, hills, wasps and mushrooms. It's the bits you don't really notice when you're going past them in a car, but if they were gone (like the sky) you'd soon want them back, in case you needed to fly somewhere quickly on holiday.

Before cities, there was no environment, because it was just where people lived and so didn't need a special long word or much looking after. But once people moved into cities and had modern inventions like front doors, the environment got left in a right state.

Poets were the first people to notice the environment. They were like an olden days version of hippies, but more annoying. A bunch of them went looking for new ideas for poems that weren't just "Ode To A Front Door," and the place they went wandering, as lonely as a clown, in their own words, was a place outside the city that we now call the environment. They saw that whales and hedgehogs and cabbages and chalk were properly getting the shitty end of the stick while humans all swanned about in those chairs on poles carried by four butlers in wigs. Something had to be done, and that something was poems.

Which is why the environment is in an absolute state to this day, because the only people who care are hippies.

In olden cities, for example, people would poo straight into the river, which meant when you drank water, you had to slosh it through your teeth like you do with jelly, to get the goodness out. Doctors soon found out that all those river poos were giving people diseases like water polo, so the first step toward the care for the environment we know today was probably making people use a toilet that went down a pipe rather than just plopping in a river. Even today it's important to put as many bleaches and chemicals down your loo as possible, to stop the sea getting infected with Victorian diseases.

In the 1980s, everyone stopped using spray cans—graffiti artists, Sigue Sigue Sputnik, the people who made custard pies for Roland Rat—to try and help repair a hole in the Oz One layer. This was so successful that the problem never reached the Oz Two layer, and today the environment is completely fine and we can pretty much relax.

It's horrible to think how bad things would be if we hadn't found out about the environment, just in time.

Evolution

The first people on Earth were animals that lived in the sea, until one of them—we don't know his name—invented legs.

The way that one animal revolves into another explains why there are so many different sorts of creature, but doesn't explain it very well. Why don't monkeys turn into crabs? If a fish can decide to have legs, why can't it decide to have four extra faces or a propeller?

So who made the rules for how animals revolve? You might think the answer is God. But, in fact, it's another old man with a beard: Charles Darling.

In 1859, in his garden in Kent, Darling saw an apple fall out of a tree and wondered, just maybe, if there was a monkey up there. And where that monkey might of come from. So Darling went on a cruise on a ship called *HMS Beatle* and collected loads of tortoises. Unlike monkeys, tortoises are really slow, so he could observe them as they evolved before his very beard.

Darling found a new hobby: thinking. You think of all sorts of weird stuff on holiday, because it's hard to get email, and your mind wanders. And when he got back home, Darling had a big circle put in his garden so he could walk round and round until he thought of something. Wandering in circles, Darling said he lost himself. But, like, it's only a circle, so you'd have to be pretty thick to get lost. Maybe that's why he was an animals scientist, not a circles scientist.

Anyway, Darling was a naturist, which is people interested in getting their bums out. And monkeys do that. And maybe that was his flash of inspiration.

This is what Darling thought: man comes from monkeys; monkeys come from fish; and fish...come from the seaside, with all seaweed and that. And turning from one creature into another had kept everyone busy for millions, even thousands of years. It was very much the internet of its day. And this idea evolved into a book.

To begin with, Darling only showed his book to his wife. And you can see why. It's really boring. I would of put loads more dinosaurs in. And maybe a high-stakes chase. On **dinosaurs.**

Because evolution can't be seen, it's hard to believe in, like **electricity**, or **skellingtons**. And because it's been around for hundreds of years, everyone it happened to is dead. Even now, humans are no closer to understanding evolution than monkeys are. But one day, maybe, we'll evolve eyes that can see evolution. And that will prove it. With our own eyes.

Until then, some people will always ask: where's the proof? Like I did at school when they made me stand by the bins. But in a way, we can see the evidence all around us, in the eye of every monkey and every dinosaur we meet. And when a caterpillar evolves into a butterfly, that's one of the most beautiful prooves there is.

Who knows what that butterfly might itself become in time? A man? A hedgehog? A supercaterpillar? Even a rainbow. And that's the miracle of life.

One thing is clear: if it weren't for evolution, *none* of us would be here today. Or we would, but we'd be gibbons. And nobody wants to be gibbons. Not even gibbons. You can tell by their bums.

Evolutionary Psychology

Evolutionary psychology is one of those important subjects that's so important that it gets professors writing **books** about it, but not so important that it gets taught at school, like maths —or lunch.

What evolutionary psychology says is that it can explain why we do things based on what we did in a previous life, when we were cavemen. This sounds brilliant at first, but it is.

So, for instance, for example, why do we jump when there's a sudden loud noise? Noises aren't scary in themselves. Noises don't have big sharp teeth or a taser or a parking ticket. But evolutionary psychology (which is much easier to type now I've cut-and-pasted it from the internet) says that we jump in case the loud noise is an exploding dinosaur. When we were cavemen, **dinosaurs** were a real danger, expecially if they were primed to blow.

We can apply this caveman-flavored thinking to all sorts of behaviors. For example, why do people run to work? You'd think it was to get in some exercise first thing in the morning, but evolutionary psychology says you're a dick if you think that. It's a tough science. People run to escape peril, so it's obvious why people run to work: because they're afraid of their homes.

And why do we clap? Is it to make a noise that indicates approval? Of course not. We clap because we like things, and we don't like getting flies on things we like, so **clapping** is the best way of killing or scaring away any flies—hence the phrase "no flies on you."

And why do we like Tizer? Is it because it's the best drink? No it isn't. (And there's no proof it is the best drink, even though it is.) It's because it reconnects us with our cavemen selves who must of drunk water from bubbling streams they'd washed their bloody hands in after hunting and killing monsters, getting a light red, bubbly liquid we associate with a job well done. (I might go out and get some Tizer.)

Evolutionary psychology can even explain things like why we hate our neighbors (in case they've moved in next door to kill us, making our homes even more frightening) and why people have children (to become so tired that death isn't such a big surprise) and I could go on, but all I can think about now is Tizer.

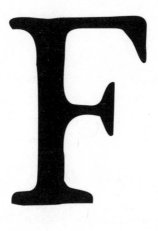

Facebook

Facebook is a sort of pub in your computer, where your mates and you can all meet and fall out with each other without having to pay for a drink or some nuts or put up with a fucking pub quiz taking place.

People tell Facebook everything, but there's one thing it can never know, and that's how someone smells. There isn't a button for having a bath or blowing off. So the people on Facebook you don't really know—you can imagine they smell like something nice, like almonds, or Glade Plug-Ins. Which'll make you like them more. But with people you've met in real life, you already know how they smell: all human and ordinary. Which makes them less mysterious.

When Facebook figures out how to do smell, everyone will be as disappointing as they *really* are. And maybe that'll be better.

Fake News

Fake news is a way of persuading people of things even though there's no evidence. Lying to you that the world is dangerous, or corrupt, or round.

Fake news used to only happen on April the first when the papers would pretend something unfunny had happened, and the presenters would read it on *BBC Breakfast* and pretend to laugh. But now it's not just one day, it's all the time. It's a worse mission creep than Christmas.

Fake news originally started on the internet. On the internet, you can lie, and there's no consequences, but if a newspaper lies on its front page, they have to print a little tiny box that says "sorry" inside a different paper weeks or sometimes years later, so that acts as a big deterrent.

Donald Trump says the mainstream media is fake news, because it says what he is doing. It's quite persuasive because most of it does sound made up, probably for a film where a bear gets to be president.

Actually, fake news is all right, really, because *real* news is quite boring. So nobody reads it. But fake news is better, because it's stuff you already think, so you don't have to read it. Just the headlines. So you have time to read more of it. Which you don't.

Farridge, Nigel

In May 2010, Nigel Farridge fell out of the sky like a shit Thor. And the world changed.

Farridge—who looks like a screaming Muppet ashtray and sounds like an after-dinner Hitler—hates unelected European politicians, despite being both a European politician and serially unelected. He's honest about this, though, and shows his contempt for his €100,000-a-year job by taking the money and hardly turning up.

Farridge says he's a man of the people. Maybe that's because he's a man, and belongs to the human race, who are people. So it's a bit of a low bar. Which is, ironically, where you'll often find him.

People like him because he's the plucky underdog. He failed to get elected to parliament in Eastleigh and Salisbury and

Battle and Thanet and Bromley and Buckingham and Thanet again. He used to be the leader of UKIP, but quit in 2015, then went back, then resigned again, then stepped back up again when the new leader resigned, then resigned again. He's a bit 52/48 about remaining or leaving.

TV producers are constantly inviting Farridge to come and shout the good news at people. And he loves the attention. It's as if he's completely insecure without a platform, like a paranoid railway station.

His archenemy is a shady group of people, a bit like the Illuminati, called the Metropolitan Elite—which sounds like a video game where you fly tube trains to distant planets to pick up artisan bread. Or a slightly tired hotel that's trying too hard but still has those little plastic thimbles of pretend milk in the rooms.

Farridge wants to defeat the Metropolitan Elite, because, like so many other ordinary decent hard-working ex-London public schoolboys who worked for the London Metals Exchange before going to work as an elite international politician and now live in West London, he can see beyond the metropolitan bubble, and good luck to him.

Fashion

Fashion is what you should be wearing for now and what you shouldn't. It's not about what you should never be wearing, like Crocs or mankinis—that's a different thing called taste. If you want to know the difference between fashion and taste, fashion changes all the time, and taste never usually does, except when they buggered up chocolate recently and made Double Deckers taste like wool.

Fashion works by making all your clothes feel disappointing after a bit. There's probably chemicals they put in new clothes that's the same chemicals that's in Turkish Delight, that makes you think you really want it, and then, like, as soon as you have it, you don't want it because Turkish Delight's rubbish. (To be honest, I'm surprised those kids stayed in Narnia as long as they did. I'd have gone back to the wardrobe and spent the afternoon trying on tops.)

Fashion these days moves pretty fast. Something you bought just a few weeks ago might now make you look like a total dick if you wear it, which is a shame, because it's probably still in one piece and perfectly OK. Maybe fashions should last longer, like tinned food or Land Rovers do.

Some things, though, never go out of fashion. Jeans is one. Everybody's got jeans except the Queen, and they haven't changed since the dawn of jeans, yet everybody's still happy to wear them except the Queen. Probably queens don't wear anything that rhymes with them—which would be why you don't see queens wearing beans or machines. She should get with the modern age and come out with her own range of Queenjeans. She could do green ones. They could have a pocket for your crown, and a change pocket that's sewn up at the top, for not carrying money.

Films

Films are a sort of **television** that's longer than one television program (say, *Bargain Hunt)* but not as long as watching all of, say, *Bargain Hunt.*

Unlike normal television, films don't come to your house unless you're not interested in them any more. You have to go and visit films where they live, which is this really big hot dog kiosk called a cinema. The hot dogs here are bigger and not as nice as the ones you can make at home using real sausages, so they take longer to eat. This means they have to give you somewhere to sit down, but because nobody likes watching strangers eat, they make all the seats face away from each other, and then, to give you something to look at, they put on a film.

Here are some films that exist.

JAWS

Some men go to sea to chase after some barrels, probably because they think there might be beer in them. The twist is that hiding under the barrels is a shark who has learned that the men love barrels, and is using them as bait. The clever shark tries to kill the men by exploding when they get near, but the men hide under the water and die, which is a lucky escape for everyone, except one of them, who luckily escapes.

FOUR WEDDINGS AND A FUNERAL

Hard to follow drama about posh people who have lots of things to go to in a row, but fortunately have loads of suits and frocks anyway, so nothing's in the cleaners, and it's not really a problem. Looked it up and apparently it's actually three weddings and a funeral and then another wedding, which makes it a bit easier to follow.

THE CANNONBALL RUN

Only seen the end. Which was brilliant. On one side of the screen is a poem made out of people's names, and on the other side of the screen is a sort of *You've Been Framed* with sex offenders. I should make clear I don't know who any of them are in the clips, and they're probably not sex offenders, but it was the 1970s and we've learned not to make assumptions.

CITIZEN KANE

Black and white.

NUNS ON THE RUN

If you've seen *The Sound of Music* or *Sister Act*, you'll know how annoying it is when a nun starts singing in a film, because it holds up the story, and the nun never gets to do a good bit like push Alan Rickman off a ledge or fight dinosaurs. This is an interesting film because it has no singing in it, but it also doesn't have any good bits, so maybe it just proves that nuns and films don't mix. A warning from God.

STAR WARS 2: STAR WARS STRIKES BACK

If you've seen the first one, *The Star Wars Menace*, this probably makes sense, but someone told me that one was hopeless, so fuck that, and I've gone straight in at what they say is the best one, and it's not. For a start, Fozzie Bear is really old in this one, and doesn't do any jokes, and they've given him Kermit's face by mistake. So someone really isn't paying attention. It ends really weird, with this Jeremy Kyle bit about who's whose dad, and then he falls down a hole, and they catch him and that's meant to be the end, even though they don't say what happens to any of them. They should do one of those bits at the end they sometimes do with old photos and some words that say which ones went to prison and who died. That or outtakes, like in *The Cannonball Run.*

THE EXORCIST

Not seen it.

CANNONBALL RUN II

Not seen it.

MANON DES SOURCES

Foreign. Not seen it.

ICE AGE 3: THE NUT JOB

Cartoon. Not seen it.

THE BRAUN ELEGANCE HAIR STRAIGHTENERS DEMONSTRATION VIDEO

Seen this loads. Hard to talk about without spoilers, but well worth getting a copy. It's never on at the cinema, but I found mine on video cassette down Barnardo's. It's my favorite film apart from *Norbit*.

NORBIT

No. Hang about. Not *Norbit*. I'm thinking of *Big Momma's House*. Not seen it.

BIG MOMMA'S HOUSE

Pretty good film.

EDWARD PENISHANDS

This is dead, dead good. Avoid the remake.

.... 🍦 ....

Frankingstein

Lots of people think that Frankingstein is the name of the monster, but it's not. It's the name of the book.

The book *Frankingstein* was written by Mary Shelley in the early 1800th century while on holiday. The **weather** was shit, so everyone she was on holiday with had to stay in and write a book, probably because they'd forgotten to pick one up at the airport.

Mary's husband was the very famous writer Mr. Shelley check name, and because he was the best known, he got to decide what game they played while they were stuck inside, even though most of them would have been happy with Pictionary. He told everyone to write a ghost story, which was a bit bossy, because Mary might have wanted to do a bonkbuster, but they all went upstairs and got their typewriters out, and Mary's was the best.

We can't remember any of the other stories, even though they were by quite famous people—plus, the others probably stuck to the brief and did ghosts, while Mary failed completely, and did mainly **electricity** and monsters. She was only a teenager at the time and if you tell a teenager to go to her room, you've only got yourself to blame if she pisses about and won't do it properly.

The book of *Frankingstein* is one of the first science fiction stories of all time, even before the old *Star Trek* where they're all in pajamas. In it, Victor Frankingstein, who's based on Doc from *Back to the Future* but traveled back to Mary Shelley times in his tin car, builds a meat robot out of bits of dead people and brings it to life by plugging it into the mains, which in those days was just a storm coming down a wire from the sky. It's amazing that a book would predict downloading stuff we needed from a cloud, but that's how good it was at science fiction.

If you don't want to read the book of *Frankingstein* because it's written in Olde English, there is a very good film version made in black and white, which is a great way to see how the monster might have looked. It's on YouTube. Just search for "Munsters," because someone's typed "Monster" wrong when they uploaded it.

···································· 🍦 ····································

Fullosophy

A great fullosopher once wrote, "Naughty, naughty; very naughty." And he knew what he was talking about because, like all good fullosophers, he spent all his time thinking—but thinking about thinking.

Human beings are the only animals who ask questions, apart from owls, who always want to know who's there. Questions like, "Is there a meaning to life?" "What am I here for?" "How did those shoes get in my fridge?" And, most weird of all, "How am I thinking these things?"

When you think about it, thinking about thinking is the hardest sort of thinking there is, which makes you think. It's probably even harder than poems or remembering the names of all the Smurfs. Luckily some people in black-and-white photograph times spent their whole lives doing exactly that sort of thinking thinking, and their brains became so *full* that they became known as *fullosophers.* The minds of fullosophers are stronger than ours because they do thinking all the time, like when you get a man to help you move a fridge. But using only thought.

The first fullosophers were ancient and Greek, and had names like Heraclitus, Petepaphides and Pythagoras. His big idea was that everything in the world could be done with numbers, like in Argos. Though, ironically, the Greek version of Argos only stocked noughts, an idea invented by some bloke called Jason. Pythagoras is best known these days as the inventor of the triangle, but a world without his ideas would be unthinkable. Because there'd be no Dairylea. And you couldn't start snooker.

Pythagoras died in 495BBC and, by then, fullosophy was all the rage. Like One Direction but with better beards: Socrates; Aristotle; Plato. They all kept their brains warm with a beard round their chin. If that's where brains is.

Plato invented Platonic relationships. Before him, men and women couldn't be just friends, they had to have sexual intercourse with each other. Which is, of course what people in platonic relationships want to do really anyway, whatever they tell you. Maybe Plato invented pretending not to want sex so he could get more of it. That'd be just like him. The devious bastard.

All that pretending not to want sex must have knackered everyone's brains, because there was no good fullosophy until Rene De Scarts was born in the sixteen hundredth century. De

Scarts is famous for saying "Cogito ergo sum," which is Latin for "I think therefore I am." It's lucky he said it in Latin, or everyone might have thought he was just Popeye. And ignored him.

What De Scarts was trying to say was: if everything is in our brains, how do we know we exist? And the answer, of course, is footprints. But how do we know our footprints are really there? What if they're somebody else's footprints? Or drawings of footprints, like at the airport? And how do we know airports is real? Most flying is in dreams, so you never know.

Friedrich Nietzsche, a German fullosopher, even tried to explain reality using the idea of Superman, which is stupid because humans can't do laser eyes or pick up skyscrapers with their bare hands. Or can they?

Trying to explain reality is so complicated that even the brainiest fullosophers can't do it in a way a normal person doesn't find really boring. Perhaps that's because thinking about thinking is a bit like singing a song about singing, or watching a TV program about a TV program, like *Extras*. In other words, not as good as the one he did first about paper.

Perhaps fullosophers should think about exciting stuff instead, like being burgled or Fireworks Night. But thinking about Fireworks Night doesn't help us understand reality. It just helps us understand fireworks. Perhaps De Scarts was right, and we think because we are. Because, if you think about it, we probably are. And if we aren't, then maybe it doesn't matter.

Unanswered Questions about Fullosophy

🦆 When people change their minds, where does the old one go?

🦆 Why don't more people just have two brains like Steve Martin?

🦆 If you think about thinking, do you use your brain or your mind? Does the brain think about the mind, so it's not too busy? What happens if the brain thinks about the brain? Does it get stuck like when you open too many windows on a cheap laptop?

🦆 Do cows get embarrassed? Is it only humans who can get embarrassed? What emotions do we think carrots are capable of? Can you shame a parsnip?

Games of Throne

Games of Throne is an epic and exciting program on the **television** and **computers** and your phone which is based on the play *King Lord of the Rings* by **William Shakespeare**. It's set in sort of series one *Black Adder* times, before dragons became extinct.

It's weird watching it because most of the time it's like medieval *Made in Chelsea* or something, just all these people getting pissed off with each other and looking serious saying loads of made up stuff in old **language**. It's so old-fashioned the script is probably given to them in the form of a tapestry. Then, just as you're getting bored with them talking and talking and walking about and talking, they have a huge spectacular fight with some zombie monsters, or a dragon monster flies down and starts having a go at them and you think maybe it was worth sitting through all the talking and then it all starts again.

You might think it's for kids, like Harry Potter, because of the dragons, but the thing is it's also got loads of tits in it, so you know it's grown-up. If there's one thing you can say about tits, it's that they're not for babies. There's so much tits in the program it's a bit like a hanging around in the ladies' changing room of some historical reenactment society. Some people say it's gratuitous but I think it's important to know women's tits looked roughly the same in fictional medieval times as they do now. They must have spent ages researching it, but it's good that someone was that thorough. It shows.

One of the main characters is called Jon Snow, but before he did the news. When he was younger he was this tortured soldier man with really nice **hair**, which is quite an achievement when you think about how hard it must be to maintain a half-decent male grooming regime by candlelight in a violent fantasy realm when you're constantly being distracted by dragons and tits.

Games of Throne doesn't just tell the story of Jon Snow off the news when he was in medieval fantastic times, it does that for loads of people. It's mainly British actors you've seen in *Midsomer Murders* and *Morse* and that, but what they were doing before, when there were dragons. So it's quite educational. If you were doing a history degree at University about what the suspects in *Midsomer Murders* were doing when they were goblins, it'd be a great way to revise. The show is so popular, that that'll probably be a round on *University Challenge* one day, or a one-off special, with Jeremy Paxman in a smock.

Game Theory

Game Theory is a way of explaining and excusing behaving like a shit because you've drawn it all out on graph paper.

The simplest way to understand it is through an idea called The Prisoner's Dilemma. First, imagine there are two prisoners. Now imagine that they have been kept in isolated rooms. Then imagine that the police have offered each prisoner the same deal: if you confess to the crime, you will get off, and your partner will go to prison for longer. Now imagine you understood any of that. That's who you are if you care about game theory.

Weird, isn't it? You've probably got a cardigan and those glasses murderers wear in black-and-white **films**.

The problem with The Prisoner's Dilemma is that it ignores real prisoners' dilemmas, which are mainly about clinging to your place in a twisted hierarchy of human bums. Any theory that ignores the real world like that probably isn't worth understanding. Which is lucky, because I don't. Besides, it ignores the currency of snouts. The person with the snouts inside is king.

(I think snouts is cigarettes, not pig face fronts. Otherwise prison is worse than I ever imagined.)

Gas

Everything is either a gas or a liquid, or not a gas or a liquid. Liquid is easy because that's water and Prosecco and Yazoo. But gas is more mysterious because you can't see it, unless it's the sort of gas with a color, like the stuff that knocks Batman out when one of the baddies squirts it in his face.

The easiest way to explain gas is with Bovril. When it's in the little pot, Bovril is a solid, like on toast. But when you add liquid, in the form of kettle water, it turns Bovril into a liquid, which you can drink, if you're not that fussed about drinking something that tastes like a McDonald's grillpan that's been left in to soak. Now, if you drew a cartoon of the horrible Bovril drink, then above the mug there would be wavy lines. These wavy lines is Bovril gas.

Nobody drinks Bovril gas, and you can't have it on toast, but that doesn't mean it isn't there, even though it's a bit hard to see and nobody really wants it. It's like *Big Brother* on Channel 5.

Gasses like Bovril gas do have their uses. You can cook with them, and you can fill up airships, if you're in black and white. Most people use electricity instead these days, which is harder to get out of Bovril. Bovril also comes in dark brown jars, which only it and Marmite do, thanks to some ancient custom like the one which says that Guinness is the only black-and-white drink or the one that says After Eights are the only thin square mint chocolates. Not that anyone's asking for more of the above.

If you use enough gas, you get a bill, which is sometimes the only evidence that the gas exists. Maybe if someone could work out how to send a bill for the Loch Ness Monster, we'd get some answers.

Genetics

Every living thing has instructions inside it for how to build it, like an IKEA Billy Bookcase. These instructions are called DNA, which is a sort of code. It took boffins ages to crack the code, even though it's fairly obvious it's just writing stuff backward, and if you solve it, it spells "AND." Not a very hard code, but scientists sometimes can't see the wood for the trees, because they're looking down a microscope.

The DNA code spells the word "and" because genetics is all about putting one thing "and" another thing together. When one person "and" another person make a baby together, the baby's genetics are a mixture of one person "and" another person, but stirred together, like when you make strawberry "and" banana Nesquik in the same cup "and" it's a whole new flavor, like banawberry. That's genetics.

DNA was discovered by two men in their 1940s in the 50s, Francis Crick, and Dr. Watson, who had stopped working for Sherlock Holmes by that time. They found that the shape of each DNA was a double helicopter, exactly as Leonard Da Vinci had originally drawn in one of his drawings hundreds of years before. When Crick and Dr. Watson won the Nobel Peace Prize for Science, Leonard Da Vinci did not get any credit, because he was dead, which remains a controversy to this day. If Leonard Da Vinci had started genetics all that time ago, we'd probably be able to not only clone a sheep by now, but put a mouse's ear on its back, and land it on the moon.

When scientists write down DNA, they do it using four letters, A, G, C and T, for some reason, even though those aren't the first letters of the alphabet, and it looks a bit like they've got distracted and started thinking about Gin and Tonic.

Every double helicopter of DNA is made of these letters in a big string. It's not clear how you get the letters into a human body. Maybe it's like a tapeworm, but made of that sticky plastic dymo stuff lonely granddads use to label stuff in sheds. A dymotapeworm.

If you copy all the letters in some DNA exactly, you can copy a whole person, which is called cloning. A clone person would be exactly the same as the original person, because their AGCTs were the same, and if they stood next to each other it would be impossible to tell the difference, like Ant and Dec when they started, or The Proclaimers. Only when one did the high bit and the other did the low bit would you be able to identify the clone Proclaimer.

I don't know why anyone would want to clone The Proclaimers, because there's already two of them. Cloning The Proclaimers is an experiment that only a madman would attempt. I reckon they should make it illegal, just in case. It would make more sense to clone someone there's only one of, like Seal, in case one of the Seals gets run over by a bus, or clubbed to death. In the future, this will be so normal, you won't even notice it, when there are two of everybody, except The Proclaimers, who there are only two of.

Governments

Governments was invented in the olden days, to stop kings doing anything they wanted, which was good because some of them did all sorts of daft bollocks, like King Kong punching that airplane, and King Rollo climbing that tree and getting all mud on his trousers.

Now, governments is typically enormous, and do everything that the ordinary man or woman in the street can't be arsed to do, from bailing out banks when they overspend to making people homeless on purpose. Some people say this is a good reason to have a small government, but that'd be no use because it wouldn't understand the needs of normal-sized people like me, and they'd make the doors too small on busses, like they do in castles, and all the coins would be like the 5p and you'd keep dropping them.

The government was a way of doing what ordinary people covered in mud wanted in all the little villages in the country. Each group of filthy yokels would choose one person, called an MP of parliament, who'd put the ideas in a bag or something, and ride on a horse to a building in the biggest village, usually London, where the ideas could be calmly debated in a metropolitan bubble. This was, until the internet was invented, the best way of having arguments about important stuff like housing, roads and who's racist.

Until you can take all the things people say under news stories on the internet and *really* turn that into law, we will have to have governments. It's not ideal, but it's better than still letting a king or queen into a position of power, which would be unthinkable in a modern 20th century country like Britain.

Gravity

Gravity is what makes things go down. Not go down like a balloon or go down like someone on Pornhub, but go down as in go down, toward the down bit of wherever the going is happening.

Gravity means that if there weren't walls in the way, and you dropped a grapefruit in Doncaster, it would keep rolling downwards until it reached Southampton. And if the grapefruit rolled onto a boat there, it would keep going until it reached Australia, where, because there's nowhere else for it to roll down to, it would stop. It's only lucky that we invented walls otherwise everything we wanted would be in Australia, and that would be really inconvenient, and some of the best things (**ice cream**, Maltesers) would melt.

Gravity was discovered by Sir Isaac Neutron and accident. He was sitting under an apple tree when an apple fell on his head. The blow to the head made him really clever and posh, like sometimes happens in cartoons, and he used that to work out what gravity was. By the time he'd had another bonk on the head, and got back to being normal again, he'd solved most of the universe. It's one of the most inspiring stories in all of science.

Nobody knows where gravity comes from. It doesn't seem to run out ever, no matter how many things we drop, so it's clearly still being made somewhere. Maybe it's best not to think about what it is or how it's made too much, and just enjoy it, like a kebab.

Great Exhibition, The

The Queen Victorians wanted to show off what they were good at, and what they were good at was showing off. So, in 1851, they built a great exhibition, and called it the Great Exhibition. (They'd had so many good ideas for steam engines, they didn't have any left for names.) It was sort of a big launch, like they have for a new Playstation, except for everything.

The Victorian Empire was so technologically advanced that it made the rest of the world look like a lump of wood. This was like the future, but a Victorian future. Which is the past. And the Queen Victorians believed their empire would last forever —so to prove that, they showed it off in a building made of the strongest substance known to man: glass.

The Great Exhibition was meant to get everyone excited about manufactured goods. It was basically the Argos catalog in a shed. Imagine a Minnellium Dome, but one that people actually wanted to go and see, and that they stored something interesting in it, rather than just the national collection of disappointed children.

The glass house and the empire are no longer there, but you can get a sense of what they must have been like by imagining you're a Victorian, and then imagining you weren't wrong about everything.

Hair

Hair is the human body's decoration. It's basically body tinsel. Most hair gathers on humans in the most important places: around the bits and coming out of the brain.

Animals have hair, too, but because they have far more of it, it's called "fur," which is the old word for "far more." (Horses have hair, because they count as human, for obvious reasons.) It's a pity fur isn't called something that reflects its nature as all-over hair, like "everywhair," but then animals don't have the same imagination as humans so they couldn't think up something as clever as that. The only animals clever enough to think of something like this are crows and dolphins, and they don't need a word for all-over hair, because they haven't got any.

Eventually, science will probably prove where hair ends and fur starts. A bit like it'll prove where sheds end and barns begin, or where mist ends and fog begins, or where shoes end and skis begin.

Hair comes in different shapes and colors. Lots of the colors are named after food, like ginger, strawberry blonde and potato brown, although I've only ever seen that last one on a box of remaindered Estonian hair dye in Poundland and they'd spelled potato with a "b." And there are almost as many hair shapes as there are hairs: perm, fade, Afro, lob, mullet— they all sound like characters from a banned children's program.

The worst hairstyles are worn exclusively by white men you wouldn't want to be trapped in a stalled train carriage with: **Donald Trump** and his golden candyfloss; Jimmy Savile and his dirty white bell; Noel Edmonds and his Dutch cottage. Elaborate and frightening crests are nature's way of warning you to keep away.

When you look at them under a microscope, hairs are surprisingly enormous, like everything. You don't realize how enormous they are usually because you take them for granted, like water and parents. Each hair has a long bit, which is the hair, and a small fat end which lives inside you, called the bollicle. Hairs drink sweat and skin oils, which is why we don't keep them as pets. Humans have up to 150,000 hairs on their head, which is enough to stretch from Trafalgar Square to Woking (or St. Albans if you've had a choppy bob).

They say if you don't wash your hair, it cleans itself. But this isn't true: what actually happens is it gets matted up and starts to smell of Wimpy, and people start moving away from you on busses, and eventually you get forced to wash it or you don't get your clothing allowance. Just ask Mick Hucknall.

Heat Death of the Universe, The

One day, experts reckon, the universe is going to just stop. The last drop of energy will run out, every single point in the whole of space will be still and lifeless and time itself will grind to a horrible halt. It'll be like working in JJB Sports in Basildon, but worse.

Apparently there's only so much energy in the universe and we're using it up every time we boil a kettle or run for a bus or burp or use a fidget spinner. There's no way of avoiding it. Even if you lagged the universe, like you do your loft, energy would leak out. It's not clear where it's leaking to, because it's the universe. Probably into a different universe, where they're absolutely cock-a-hoop, like when you can get your neighbor's wi-fi.

But everything is sort of slowing down.

Imagine the start of the universe was a big Monday with loads to do, and we're heading toward an inevitable Sunday afternoon where everyone's full of roast and crumble and the *Antiques Roadshow* is on and you can't really be arsed to do a thing. That's how it all ends. With every single atom in the universe slumped half-watching pensioners in car coats queuing outside Beaulieu Motor Museum to meet a man in a waistcoat who knows everything in the world about Toby jugs. That's what we've got to look forward to. It's enough to make you chuck it in.

Henry of Eight

After Henry of Seven came to the end of his reign in 1509, he regenerated into Henry of Eight—the big one. The Tom Baker of kings. He's the one, if you drew a king, you'd definitely do. Him or King Kong.

Henry of Eight enjoyed standing with his legs apart, bellowing and writing catchy but repetitive songs—a sort of Tudor Status Quo. If you've ever rung a doorbell in Basildon, you'll know his stuff.

He had eight wives, all called Catherine, so he wouldn't shout the wrong name in bed. He was a Catherine-aholic, sometimes shortened to "Catholic." His first wife was Catherine of Aragon. He returned her to the church because she wasn't working properly and couldn't make a baby—just like you'd return dodgy hair straighteners to Argos. His second wife, Catherine of Anne Boleyn, worked a bit better, and nearly did a baby, but Henry fell off a horse and the shock stopped her working. Henry lost his rag with her, and started having it off with Catherine of Jane Seymour. And just so Catherine of Anne Boleyn wouldn't notice, he cut her head off.

Catherine of Jane Seymour was the first of his wives who worked properly, and she gave birth to a son, Prince Edward, in the year 1537 and her bed. Sadly, as soon as she became a mum, she stopped working properly and died twelve days later. Henry was distraught, but had to find another wife; and he found one in a painting of Catherine of Anne of Cleves. Her name was Catherine of Anne of Cleves. She turned out to be a bit of a Disprin, so the marriage was dissolved.

With Henry's chronic wife addiction left untreated, he got another one: Catherine Howard. She was too much like him—always having it off elsewhere—so he had her head cut off to make her less attractive to other men, and married Catherine Parr instead.

But all Henry's flip-flopping between women had caused problems with the Pope, who didn't like Henry dumping his wife every time there was a new bit of skirt in town. So Henry basically dumped the Catholic Church and started seeing a new one: The Church of England. And, although he never married the CofE (probably because it wasn't called Catherine) he had an affair with it for the rest of his life.

By the end of his life, Henry was almost completely spherical. Kings in those days ate loads, and Henry's kitchens at Hampton Court Palace were the fucking nuts. Unfortunately, he eventually ate so much that he basically burst.

So what was so great about Henry of Eight? Why is he the king we all know about, unlike, say, Richard V or King Crimson? Well, for a start he was fat. And fat people are always more memorable than thin ones, because they take up more room in the memory: that's why we all still remember Father Christmas even though he's dead. And Henry was memorable because he was randy. When he wasn't eating himself massive, he was having it off. He was a sort of cross between Augustus Gloop and Russell Brand.

He also had a zany sense of humor. He ate peacocks for the hell of it and once had a man boiled to death. And he left behind two amazing properties—the biggest garden in Britain: Richmond Park, which is still full of the ancestors of the deers that he was too fat to hunt properly—and Hampton Court Palace, a theme park dedicated to himself, like Disneyworld with harpsichord music.

Henry of Eight was the kingiest king there has ever been. It's hard to imagine there being another Henry of Eight, probably because we'd have to call him Henry 8S or Henry 9 or Henry X or whatever.

.... 🎞 ....

Hiccups

One of the strangest things the human body can do is to hiccup (or, to use the correct medical term, "do a hiccup").

Science has struggled to explain hiccups for many months. There are theories, like that it's the body's alarm clock going off, or that it's a small internal organ left over from when we were frogs that sounds off now and then, but doesn't mean there's anything to worry about, like a fire alarm drill in an office that everybody ignores every Friday.

But if hiccups were like a fire alarm drill, how would you know when they were a real fire alarm, and that you should run screaming from the human body because it's on fire? That's another question that science hasn't got round to answering, along with "What's the difference between a cold and a chill?" and "How do you clean cheese off the joints of a sandwich toaster?"

Perhaps there's a clue to what hiccups is in the word "hiccups." The "hic" bit is obviously the noise, but what's the "cups"? Nobody knows. So perhaps there's not a clue to what hiccups is in the word "hiccups." Perhaps I'm wrong.

Perhaps I've been wrong about everything. Perhaps this whole book is a waste of time. Maybe all the time I've been dictating this into my phone, I could have been doing something worthwhile, like asking it to play songs about doctors. Why aren't there more songs about doctors? You'd think people would want them, but I can only think of about one. Or maybe none. You'd think there'd be more. The world's amazing like that. Anyway, that's hiccups.

Human Mind, The

One of the most mysterious journeys that science has ever taken isn't through the sea, or into the Moon, but down behind the human face, into the brain.

The brain makes up around 2 percent of an average human's body weight, which means that if you are thinner than average, a bigger proportion of your body is made up of brain. This is why we listen to what famous people like actors say, because generally they are thinner, and therefore cleverer than the rest of us.

The brain is the most complexated part of the body. Compared to the brain, your hand might as well be your bum. That's how complexated the brain is.

To understand the brain, imagine a cauliflower. Which looks a bit like a brain. Because you're imagining a cauliflower, your brain is now, like, a cauliflower, but with another cauliflower inside: a thought cauliflower.

How that thought cauliflower got there is amazing. The human brain contains millions of small bits called neurons that store ideas, called ideas. If you could take the top off your head without dying or getting leaves on your brain, you'd see little bits of lightning all moving about on the cauliflowery bit, which are what ideas look like, except to see in the top of your own head you'd have to put your eyes on a sort of selfie-stick and that might stop them working.

These tiny bits of lightning can join together, so that small, simple ideas (pointing your finger, say) can become bigger, more complex, layered ideas (let's open a shop over there where I'm pointing that sells upcycled clocks made out of old dialysis machines, because that's the sort of hipster rubbish that sells quite well these days, and it might make a little bit of money, but hang on, where would we get a load of old dialysis machines, and it's probably really hard to make clock mechanisms and I don't really have the skills or the tools, and actually I've not really thought this through, maybe I'll just pretend I was pointing at the Chicken Cottage, so if I say let's go to Chicken Cottage, we could just go and get some dippers and I quite fancy dippers, but haven't I got that leftover macaroni cheese in the fridge I opened when I was drunk and I should probably just eat that, so maybe dippers is a bad idea, and now I'm just standing pointing, and I'm not sure I can style this out, oh good, a pigeon, I'll pretend I was pointing at the pigeon and nobody has to get any dialysis machines or dippers and we've made a lucky escape there, look, a pigeon) and that's the brain doing what it does best.

And the mystery doesn't stop at the brain, because inside the brain is an even bigger mystery: the human mind. You can't see the mind, or touch it, or taste it, though if you could taste it, it would probably taste like a cross between a cauliflower and something magical, like Baked Alaska or I Can't Believe It's Not Butter.

The mind is said to contain everything we are. Think about that for a minute. Now stop, because it doesn't make sense. Everything we are is a big fucking deal. Some of what we are is in there: our memories, our dreams, our PIN numbers.

But a lot of what we are isn't in our minds. Our driving licenses aren't in our minds. Our saucepans aren't in our minds. Our hairdressers aren't in our minds. (Unless you've got an imaginary hairdresser, like kids have imaginary friends. That's not such a bad idea. It'd be someone to tell about your holidays, if no one at work was interested, I suppose.)

Boffins who have studied the mind using their own minds have come to some grim conclusions: either that the human mind isn't capable of understanding the human mind, or that understanding the human mind causes a human's mind to blow.

But how can the human mind be so confusing to the human mind? After all, the human mind can understand some of the most absurdly complexated things, like tennis and recipes and insurance. Perhaps it's a shortcoming of the human body—a bit like how you'll never look yourself in the eyes, or taste your own tongue, or rest your head gently on your own chest and cry your heart out about how you'll never taste your own tongue.

Plenty of people have wasted their time trying to understand the human mind. And not just scientists and Einsteins, either. Fullosophers, who are like scientists (but scientists who don't bother actually doing anything) have for centuries asked questions about what the mind is for, and never come up with any proper answers, so maybe that answered their question: it's for thinking about proper things, like whether you want dippers, not all that rubbish, which it can't do at all.

A French fullosopher called Renny De Scarts came up with a famous quote: "I think therefore I am," which, even though it's not as good as "I'll be back" or "Bazinga," and so isn't on as many stickers and mugs, has remained quite popular even though he never finished it and said what he therefore was. Maybe it's popular because you can finish it yourself, with whatever you like: "I think therefore I am hungry," or "I think therefore I am Adam Woodyatt." It leaves space for you to think your own thinks, which is what the brain is for.

It's amazing to think that a million years ago we couldn't use our brains to read or write, because we just thought about **dinosaurs** and grunting. So in another million years, who knows what we'll be able to do with our brains? Maybe we'll be able to tell what card someone's thinking of, or bend spoons, or saw a lady in half. Our brains might be so advanced that we could actually imagine everything. Imagine that.

Perhaps one day, a mind will be grown big enough to understand the human mind. Until then, it remains a beautiful cauliflowery mystery, like the whereabouts of Lord Lucan or the success of Simon Cowell.

Ice Cream

In the olden days, things was simpler. Ice cream came in one flavor: plain. Then boffins discovered raspberry ripple, which at the time was like the **Large Hadron Colander** discovering whatever it is it's looking for. To be honest they should set the Hadron thing looking for new ice cream flavors. But then I suppose Switzerland's mainly yogurt, so they've not got the heritage.

Plain ice cream came in two types: the one you got in the shops, which was standard issue yellow, and the one you got on the street, which was white. Ice cream is probably the only food to roam the streets in vans looking for consumers. It's weird that such a popular food should be so needy. You'd think it'd be the unpopular foods that needed to be hawked round the streets. Maybe if there was Brussels sprouts vans, we'd all like them more.

Ice Cream Accessories

Most people like to pimp their ice cream with something. The most common accessory is the *Flake*. If you add a Flake to an ice cream (though it's only half a Flake, actually) it's called a 99, because no matter how many problems you've got, the ice cream isn't one of them. The next most common is *Sprinkles*, which used to be called Hundreds And Thousands, before the EU counted them and realized there were billions in existence, but only a few dozen on every ice cream, so outlawed the term. *Sauce* is allowed, especially chocolate and strawberry, but mainly strawberry. Things not to pimp your ice cream with include UV lights, go-faster stripes and alloys.

Then, in the 1980s, the world of ice cream went absolutely fucking berserk. The Viennetta came out. No one had ever seen anything like it before, not even in their dreams. It was what ice cream would look like on its wedding day. Suddenly ice cream was big news. It made everyone forget the IRA and AIDS and now if you look at the history pages on the internet, they're never about 1980s wars or politicians, they're mainly about the history of Viennetta!*

Nowadays, anything is allowed in ice cream, the weirder, the better: salt, tequila, even mustard—that maniac Charlton Heston Blumenthal made a mustard ice cream, just in case anyone wanted to put the tin hat on a nice dinner by being sick everywhere.

··

Industrial Revolution, The

The Victorians invented something that was to change the world, and that something was something called steam. Steam is what you get when you make water absolutely furious. It's hot, unpredictable, powerful and lethal, like Mel Gibson.

The Victorians used steam to power huge engines, which could be put in factories, trains and the Science Museum. Before steam, all the hard work had to be done by horses. But unlike horses, steam could be pumped along pipes and stored in kettles without upsetting the RSPCA.

Now the Victorians had big engines, they could build big factories. Huge places, full of noise and machinery and with only the most basic break-out spaces and no wi-fi.

* if you type "Viennetta" in

People worked twelve- to fourteen-hour days with no lunch break and had to clean their own equipment and were sometimes even attacked by their bosses—conditions unthinkable to anyone these days who doesn't work for the NHS. You could be fined for talking, whistling or leaving the room—it was like one really big, super-serious GCSE. Workers were even punished by having their ears nailed to the table: something unimaginable now, when it's only willies that are nailed to things—and not for punishment, but for funishment.

The rise in industrialization meant a rise in poverty too. Changes in the way things were made—by machines, not people—put many out of work. Say you used to make furniture for a living: well, now there were machines that did that. So you were out of a job. And the only job you could get was making a machine that made furniture. Except there aren't any machines that look like chairs or poufs, so your skills were useless. You could try getting a job as a machine, but machines were better qualified, and worked longer hours. Even traditional trades like Jack the Ripping were threatened, by newfangled person-killing machines like the train crash. In the end everyone had to become a chimney sweep or a Scrooge or an urchin, because there weren't any machines that could do those jobs. It was horrible.

Transport was upgraded during the Industrial Revolution. Roads were improved so they didn't get waterlogged, and special very waterlogged roads called canals were built. And, of course, there was the railway. The railway made moving things by train easier than before, when there were trains but no railway.

Trains could take stuff huge distances, and they worked much harder and faster than horses. Unlike horses, they had big smiling faces on the front, and the voice of Ringo Starr. It might seem cruel to have worked them so hard, but these jolly creatures didn't mind it. You could say the train was the most revolutionary animal that mankind had ever domesticated, until the Furby.

One of the things the railway could move was people, into cities from out in the countryside where they used to be farmers or horses or smallholders, which is people that don't have much. And once people moved into the cities, they came face-to-face with the reality of the metropolitan elite lifestyle: overcrowding, slums, workhouses, lack of sanitation, cholera and enormous hats.

Industry took advantage of all the latest inventions: the telegraph, very much the internet of its day, the telephone, very much the internet of its day, and the typewriter and the postage stamp, which combined were very much the internet of their day.

It didn't last, of course. Soon the Industrial Revolution stopped industrially revolving, and people rediscovered the joys of nature, by moving all the industrial units into fields near main roads in the countryside, where they were closer to the garden center. These days, no one works in these factories and mills except ghosts, and even then, they only work night shifts.

But without the Industrial Revolution, we wouldn't have bicycles and tins of beans, and IKEA would be literally empty. We'd all be riding around in handmade busses catching fish and making our own entertainment, and instead of Twitter there'd be a scarecrow competition. It'd be completely shithouse.

······················· 🕐 ·······················

iPhone, The

In the olden days, when phones were young, they were big things with bells in them and a massive sort of Spirograph arrangement of numbers, and they were actually part of a building: attached to the wall, or built into a cast iron on-street toilet cubicle. Then, as they grew up, they left home, like people do, and you could carry them in your pocket. And then, as they got old, they got smaller, like people do. And then, like people do, they died.

When phones died was when a completely new phone was born. And that phone was the iPhone. It had a small letter at the front, just like the word "phone" always did, but a big letter next, signifying that this was something important, like a famous person or a Volvo.

The iPhone wasn't just a phone: it was also a camera and a diary and a **television** and an address book and a notepad and an atlas and a radio and a torch and a calculator and a clock and a hi-fi and a cupboard full of games and a pile of remote controls and a minicab office and a bookshop and a fitness instructor and a tour guide and a translator and a **weather** forecaster and a travel agent and a genius. It was like a cross between the contents of a school bag and everything else in the world.

This was a device which revolutionized our attention spans, crushing them down smaller than ever before. Now we didn't need to be drunk to walk straight into lamp-posts. Now we didn't need to pay attention to the TV any more. Now we could have conversations with people miles away from the comfort of the cinema. Now we could sharpen our reflexes by only noticing the car in front had stopped at the last minute when we looked up from **Facebook**.

But though the iPhone was the biggest new invention since, I don't know, wood or something, it couldn't do everything—and even though I've suggested it to the guy at Carphone Warehouse every time I've been in, there still isn't an app that can tell me how many crisps there are in a packet.

Obviously, like everyone, I've memorized the important ones —53 in a packet of Hula Hoops, 25 in a packet of Quavers, 17 in a packet of Monster Munch, 31 in a packet of Mini Cheddars and 42 in a packet of Wotsits—but what happens when there's only own brand crisps in the shop, or if I'm at the pub and they've got those posh ones with pictures of fields and ingredients on them? That's when the app CunkCrispCount would come in vitally handy. It could even save a life. Imagine someone was allergic to more than ten Doritos and they didn't know there are fifteen in a packet—those last five could be the difference between a delicious mouthful of Chili Heatwave and death.

.... 🕐 ....

Iron Age, The

The Iron Age came about when primitive cave-boffins discovered new materials. Early man dropped rocks like a stone, and got into metal, bronze and then iron. Iron Man was born.

This Iron Man didn't have superpowers like the Iron Man in **films**—he couldn't fly or tolerate Gwyneth Paltrow — so instead he had to go to lengthy measures to defend himself. Luckily cave-boffins had also invented the iron spike. And shortly after inventing the spike, they invented stabbing each other.

To make sure they stabbed the right people, Britons formed into primitive gangs, called tribes. It was war. But crap war. Iron Man didn't just do violence, he painted himself blue first, like a Millwall fan. He wasn't a nice blue man like the Blue Man Group or Avatar or Mr. Bump, but angry and blue, like a rabid Smurf.

But their faces weren't the only things that were outrageous and blue. There was also hills. Iron Age hills were just covered in huge drawings of men with colossal prongs. You didn't know where to look.

Before Snapchat, hills were the most efficient way to distribute cock pics to a wide audience. The hill was very much the

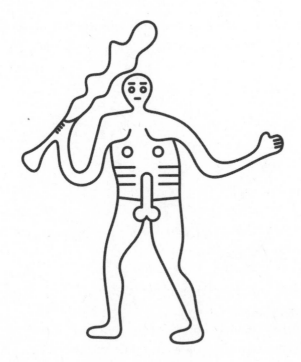

The Cerne Abbas Giant

internet of its day. These NSFW hills can still leave you open-mouthed. This one, the Cerne Abbas Giant, would remain Britain's biggest hillside dick, until 2009, when Chris Moyles trained to climb Mount Kilimanjaro—and it remains the second crudest Hill in British history, after Benny.

There's disagreement about how old the Cerne Abbas Giant actually is, especially since he's still young enough to get wood.

What's not in doubt is that he represents the birth of British art, being the biggest example of a noble visual tradition that's echoed down the ages.

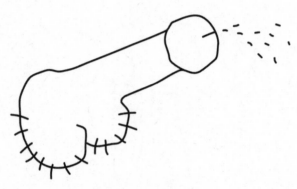

Traditional British art

Fun fact: nobody knows where Iron Man found the iron. Maybe it was in the cupboard under the stairs. That's where mine usually is.

.... 💀 ....

Jazz

Jazz is sort of music, but clever. It's not as clever as classical, which you need exams to understand, but it's a lot cleverer than, say, grime or Coldplay.

Jazz was discovered in America in the early 20th century, hiding inside the blues, which was sad songs sung by people who'd been made slaves. Slaves are a sort of worker who's only paid once, and the money's given to someone else. This arrangement made them so sad they played songs on a guitar, because they couldn't afford orchestras, on a porch, because they couldn't afford wherever it is orchestras live.

The main thing about jazz is that it's made up. All music is made up, but usually only once—you write the song, and then you sing it. Jazz is different. It's made up every time you play it, which must be exhausting and is possibly a waste of notes. There are only so many notes in the world, and one day they're going to start to run out. Future generations might see jazz in the same way we now see plastic—a terrible waste of resources, tipping loads of notes into landfill, polluting the planet with saxophone solos and trumpet noises. Hopefully science will one day work out a way to recycle notes, perhaps into new music, hopefully not for Sting.

Saxophones and trumpets are very much the bread and spread of jazz. Also common are the trombone (which looks like a cross between a trumpet and a rocket launcher), the double bass (a violin for giants) and the piano (you know what a piano is, so I'm not looking that one up). There are some instruments that aren't allowed to do jazz by law, like the harp, the xylophone and the church organ. Jazz on any of these would sound frankly ridiculous, and the jazz police would come down on them like a ton of police.

Jazz even has its own language. It's called scat, and you definitely shouldn't Google it. I don't even want this millionaire's shortbread now.

Famous jazz people include Ellie Fitzgerald, Dave Brewdog and HRH The Duke of Ellington.

Jesus

Jesus (full name Jesus Christ) is famous because he gave his name to two separate things to shout when a bus drives straight past you at the stop without stopping (his nearest competitor Gordon Bennett only got one). He was also one of the most important men who ever lived, if he did, which he did. In many countries, we even count our dates from when he was born, and the "C" in BC is for "Christ," which shows how important he was.

Christ was born around 4BC, four years before the birth of Christ, in the oh little town of Bethlehem, in what is now one of the countries they have on that map on the news all the time. Jesus's mother was Mary, a professional virgin, and his two dads were Joseph, a carpenter, and God, an all powerful mega-being. It's amazing that Mary and him got on. They had nothing in common, and the power dynamic would have been very one-way. It's a bit like when you go out with a teacher. It's just wrong.

The Romans, who were in charge in BC times, said Joseph had to go to do some paperwork. In those days there wasn't much paper, so you had to walk miles to find it. When Joseph and his little donkey got to the town where the paper was, there was no room for Mary to lay her baby, but an innkeeper shoved them all outside, and soon Jesus was eventually born in a stable condition.

We know about Jesus's life and what he said and what he was like because it was written down in the Bible. And luckily for us, it wasn't just written down one time, but four times, contradicting each other, by some people who met him (and some who didn't) about thirty to seventy years after he'd died, which is the best way to get the facts straight when you write a book about anybody.

When I read *Straight Up* by **Danny Dyer**, I kept thinking to myself, this would be much better if instead of Danny Dyer writing about stuff that was happening to him and what he thought, four different people who weren't Danny Dyer didn't write about Danny Dyer at all yet, but waited until about the year 2060, and then tried to remember what Danny Dyer thought and did and was like, and that was the book instead. I think that would be, if it's possible to believe such a thing, an even better book than *Straight Up* by Danny Dyer. This is no disrespect to Danny Dyer. I'd like to stress that *Straight Up* by Danny Dyer is one of my favorite books I've ever read, and I'm looking forward to finishing it.

Unlike Danny Dyer, Jesus never appeared in the film *Run For Your Wife*, or *EastEnders*. Instead he did the next best thing for the times. He stood on hills and told people off. It's hard to imagine, but centuries before the invention of radio or the channel Dave Ja Vu, and nearly two thousand years before the painting and decorating sitcom **Brush Strokes**, this was all there was. People came from miles around and got well into it. In a way, standing on hills and telling people off was very much the internet of its day.

If you want to get an idea of what it would have been like to go and see Jesus standing about and telling strangers off, you can go to any shopping precinct, where his followers do the same to this day, often into megaphones. What made Jesus different than someone shouting outside Claire's Accessories is that he was not probably a bit mad. Jesus proved he wasn't mad by saying he was the son of God, could walk on water, and raise the dead. And over ten people heard him and followed him (twelve). It's easy to see why he changed the world.

He changed water into wine, rode a little donkey, chased some money out of a temple, taught a blind man to see and fed five thousand loaves to some fish, inventing the fish finger. He also cured some disabled people. He did this by telling them their sins were forgiven, and once they had been forgiven of these bad things that they had done, they could walk again. Because to Jesus, who was meek and kind, not being able to walk was definitely your own fault. By simply purging people of bad thoughts and deeds, their illnesses and weaknesses were cured. Philosophically he was very much somewhere between Katie Hopkins and Noel Edmonds.

Eventually, those over ten people following Jesus became a proper pain in the arse to the Romans, who wanted everyone to believe in their gods—Hercules, Asterix, Quasimodo—rather than the Father, Son and Holy Spirit: the single god of the Christian religion.

The Romans tricked one of Jesus's followers—Judas (whose name means "he who can do Judo")—into doing exactly what

Jesus wanted, and he betrayed him by snogging him in a park, which brought the Romans down on him like a ton of bricks. Judas is hated to this day by all Christians, because if he hadn't betrayed Jesus, Jesus would never have been nailed to a cross by the Romans, and could have lived forever. Instead of a cross, Christians would have to wear a little model of a man being fine and just getting on with stuff and getting old. It's not as good a logo, so I think Judas gets pretty shoddy treatment here. Christianity took the world by storm, and Judas's influence on the branding can't be underestimated.

After Jesus was killed by the Romans, he [SPOILERS] came back from the dead, like Freddy Krueger. But instead of cutting everybody up with scissors fingers, he flew up into the sky, where he lives to this day, with his dad. It's unusual for a father to get custody, but that's God for you.

Because of Jesus's life and sacrifice, he saved every person on Earth. Jesus was the only son of God, and it's quite nice that he sent his only son to this planet, rather than any of the other planets in the whole of his creation, because there are billions, apparently. It's nice to think that wherever E.T. lives, and however much he cares for plants and opens the hearts of little boys, that little alien will burn in hell for all eternity, because he didn't get a Jesus. There is only one. And we got him. Screw you, squashy.

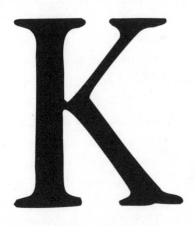

King Arthur

King Arthur was the greatest king of England that never existed. At the age of fifteen, he pulled a non-existent sword called Excalibur out of a made-up stone and became king. In those days, you had to qualify.

He lived in a castle called Camelot, which he didn't because it didn't exist, and had a wizard called Merlin except he didn't and invented a round table, which was a sort of lazy Susan, which meant his knights could get at the snacks they wanted without having to move around in their armor, except they and the table weren't there either.

Some of the imaginary knights went off to look for a holy cup, which isn't a thing. One of them went mad and became a hermit crab, and one of them died—even though they didn't.

When he knew he was dying, which he wasn't because he wasn't real, he gave his non-existent sword to Sir Bedevere, who wasn't there, who threw it into a lake someone thought of where a lady's hand that was nothing of the sort caught it.

It might be a load of bollocks, but it's a cracking good story, and without it we wouldn't have Roxy Music's *Avalon* or *Monty Python's Life Of Brian*. It's hard to imagine Britain at all without the existence of King Arthur. But because he didn't exist, we have to. Which is maybe why we are where we are today, wherever that is.

.... 🌍 ....

King Isambard of Brunel

King Isambard of Brunel was one of the best engineers of the Victorians times. He constructed bridges, tunnels and boats as well as the largest freestanding top hat in Britain. If anyone needed to get anywhere, Brunel would change how they did it, whether it was to America by boat, across the Thames by tunnel, into Bristol by bridge, or under a low doorway by top hat.

Brunel's most famous boat was the *Great Britain*, so called because it weighed as much as Great Britain. It wasn't made of wood, that floats on water, like a boat, but iron, that doesn't. This was because Brunel had worked out that the most famous boats are the ones that sink, and his name would live forever if he made one of those. He wasn't wrong, and even though his boat didn't sink, we all still think it should of, and now everyone knows the name King Isambard of Brunel.

Sadly he didn't leave an heir, and a revolution in the kingdom of Brunel meant he was its last ever king. ☹

Language

Human beings are, as far as we know, the only creatures to have evolved a complex verbal language to communicate ideas, except Smurfs. But while the Smurf language only has one word for everything ("smurf") the human language has words for all different things, which has made it possible for us to dominate the whole planet, not just a little cluster of toadstool houses.

Not only does human language have words for everything, it has loads of different words for everything depending on where you live. For example, what the English call "a chauffeur" is called *"un chauffeur"* in France, our word "table" is their word *"table"* (but with a shrug and a cigarette), and if you tried to order an Eau De Cologne in a French restaurant, you'd have a great deal of trouble making yourself understood at all. Believe me, I've tried.

The many different languages make it much easier for humans not to understand each other, which is a great help to both arms manufacturers and racists. Several idiots have tried to develop a universal language, but everybody would have to learn it, and that seems a bit of a faff when most foreign-language-speakers are quite happy putting up with British people just talking a bit louder and pointing.

Scientists have studied whether humans learn language or are born with it. But they haven't studied it very hard because anyone who's ever done a long train journey knows babies only have one word and it's screaming. They're like a little one-person hen party. That's not language. If they were born with language you wouldn't have to keep saying words to them very slowly in a head-injury voice and pointing at things, like a British tourist trying to buy soap.

Scientists who study this sort of thing are called linguists and probably feel a bit stupid at scientist parties when they have to make small talk with people who look for black holes and cures for stuff. "What do you study?" "Words." "Isn't that just reading slowly?" Yes. Yes it is.

Large Hadron Colander

The Large Hadron Colander is the most expensive colander ever built. It is also the largest. If you want to colander some hadrons, there is no larger place. The thing about hadrons is they're quite large, hence the name, and you need lots of room. Hadrons simply won't fit into a smaller colander. They're not like peas.

The Large Hadron Colander was built in Switzerland, because they are the world's experts on colander holes, thanks to their longstanding work on the holes in cheese. The holes in this colander are the best they can be. They don't let any of the hadrons out, to roll all over the floor and under cupboards. The holes in the colander really are the Ferrari of holes. They make the holes in the colander you might have in your kitchen look like a horse and cart.

The Large Hadron Colander costs over £700m a year to keep running. That might seem a lot, but once you understand what they're doing it makes more sense, I'd imagine. It must be important, or they wouldn't do it. Maybe the ordinary layman has trouble conceiving of how bad things would be in the world if all those hadrons weren't put in a colander, but that doesn't mean the boffins should stop. Good luck to them, I say. It's not my money.

Unless it is. In which case, stop.

Maybe it would help if we understood what a hadron was, but I've looked it up, and it just made my head hot. I think we're going to have to trust the eggheads on this one. Unless it's my **money** of course. Maybe we should all check our bank statements. If you see a bill for colanders or science that you weren't expecting, have a word.

> ### Unanswered Questions about
> ### the Large Hadron Colander
>
> If I paid for it, can I ride in it?
>
> Would it be a good idea to spend the same money again to build something else just as good but something that ordinary people understand? Like a water slide? How good would that be?
>
> Isn't it time we left hadrons alone?

Lies

Lies are meant to be bad, and in the Bible they're one of the worst things you can do that doesn't involve an ox. Even though we all know lies are wrong, lots of people tell lies for a living: magicians, actors, **Donald Trump**.

Magicians tell nice lies, like "I can read your mind." Actors do too: they pretend to be other people. Adam Woodyatt isn't really Ian Beale, even though it's literally the only thing he's done his entire adult life. You could say Adam Woodyatt's whole life has been a nice lie, for him, and—in a lesser sense—for us.

Donald Trump has a different definition of lying from most other people, just like he has a different definition of sexual assault, or thinking, or **hair**. When he lies, he points at other people and says they're lying instead, to try and draw attention away from what he's doing, a bit like pointing at a really fat person because you want to distract people from the fact that you've shat your pants.

Maybe truth went out of fashion because so many liars got away with ignoring it. Richard Nixon, Billary Clinton, Jeffrey Archer and maybe worst of all, Lance Armstrong. Lance Armstrong had been an American hero. But it turned out he'd been lying. It was hard to know what was worse: that he'd taken shedloads of drugs, or that he'd never actually been to the Moon.

Maybe the worst liar ever was the wooden puppet Pinocchio. Every time he lied, his film got longer. Or at least that's how it felt when I had to watch it with my niece.

Light

Light is the fastest animal in the world, even faster than a cheetah. Some scientists say that light isn't an animal, but ask them what light actually is, and they can't tell you. Believe me, I've tried. They haven't got a Scooby. They just start arguing about whether light is particular or waving or God knows what and you glaze over and wished you'd asked something else.

All things are either animal, vegetable or mineral. We know light is not a vegetable, because it's not green (except green lights, and even they change, which vegetables don't) and it's not a mineral, because it's not made of rocks, so light is obviously an animal. This theory is mine, and if any scientists would like to adopt it, they are welcome to as long as they remember to name it after me and spell my name right.

Light is not only the fastest animal, it's also one of the smallest. It can fit into your eye, like a spider, and get under doors, like a mouse. But you can tell it isn't a spider or a mouse because it has a different number of legs (none).

Light is so fast that a speed has been named after it: "the speed of light." The speed of light is what is known as a "constant." This means it is the same everywhere, like McDonald's, and so light travels at exactly the same speed anywhere you go in the whole universe, except underwater, where it's different.

To help understand light without worrying about if you're underwater, scientists measure it in a vacuum. Light isn't the only animal that can be measured in a vacuum. Hamsters, for example, are quite easy to measure in a vacuum too. If you've got a load of hamsters running around in a room, and you hoover them up, you can count them a lot easier once they're in the bag. It's another bit of evidence for light being an animal. Copyright me.

Light turns out to be made up of lots of different colors, like Smarties. If you want to see the colors, you need to get a special triangular wedge of glass cheese called a prison. If you put light into the prison, it turns into a rainbow, which is a lot cheerier than what happens to people when you put them in a prison. But then most glass triangles aren't full of 18-stone psychopaths who've been secretly sharpening a toothbrush to use on someone called Billy Eyeball in the laundry.

The seven colors that light breaks into are called red, orange, yellow, green, blue, purple and purple again, making six colors in total. The easy way to remember the order of these colors is to write it down somewhere.

The glass cheese light rainbow was discovered by the inventor of **gravity**, Sir Isaac Neutron. He experimented on light by ramming a pointed stick into his eye and found that he could see loads of colors, which was about as surprising as his discovery that if you sit under an apple tree what eventually falls on your head is an apple. When you think about it, it must have been dead easy to discover stuff before all the stuff was discovered, and it's much harder now, which is why my theory about light being an animal is even more amazing, because there's less obvious stuff to just say was your idea now, and you have to think outside the box a bit.

Longitude

All maps of the world are drawn on big graph paper, with squares, because squares is the best way to divide up a round thing like a globe.

To help sailors and airplane drivers know which square they are on, the lines have numbers. The ones from top to bottom are called latititude, and it's easy to tell which square you are on just by looking around you, because the countries change a lot as you move from the top to the bottom of the world. Spain is different from the North Pole, for instance, and has a totally different number of penguins.

But working out where you are side to side—longitude—is harder, because those countries are sort of the same, and nobody can really tell which one's Denmark and which one's Holland without asking, and when you do ask, the answer just sounds like the Swedish chef from the Muppets, which is hopeless.

In Pirate Ship times this was a big problem. Also you couldn't tell where you were on the map because nobody had mobile phones that could just ring up a stalactite navigation system in orbit and ask it what was your GPS. In those days, phones were huge like they used to have on *Saturday Superstore*, with those curly wires, and they were nailed to the wall of your house, so it was no use if you were in a different country or the sea.

Eventually someone did work it out, using a clock. They'd set the clock when they left the harbor to show breakfast time. Then they would know which country they were in by looking at when people had breakfast. In London, it would be quite early, because the trains are shit and you have to leave a bit before you want to in case there's signaling problems. But in France, they'd loaf around in bed with strangers, having sex and smoking until about eleven, so breakfast would be later. By checking when local toasters popped up, sailors would know where they were. And that's the magnificent story of longitude.

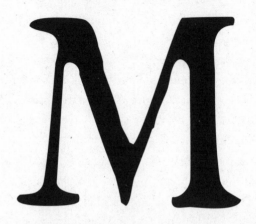

Medicine

For thousands of years, man has been getting better, thanks to one single thing: medicines. Medicines means we can treat everything from made-up diseases like the plague, to modern epidemics like allergicness to bread.

The word "medicine" comes from the Latin word "*medicina*," which means "medicine A," or "first medicine." Before this first medicine, people believed that sickness was caused by evil spirits, like Freddy Krueger, so it was a relief to find that what caused people to be ill could be killed without requiring sequels. The ancient Egyptians thought that onions were medicine, but they're not. They're onions.

In the olden days, one way of medicine was to release the bad ghosts by drilling a hole in someone's head. This is why people today have nostrils. To let the ghosts out, in the form of a sneeze. And that's why it's important to say "bless you." Otherwise you might go to hell.

Medicine comes in many forms. Some go inside, like tablets and injections, and some go outside, like bandages and oinkment. There's also surgery, where they take what was inside and make it outside. And no matter how much you want to, you're not allowed to do that one yourself. Most medicines have a scientific name, like Domestos, and a short nickname that's easy to remember, like E. The people who do medicine are doctors. Doctors live in big houses called Bedside Manors. In a place called Medical Essex.

In other countries and the past, only rich people can afford to get better, but in this country, there is the National Health Surface, which means everyone can get better if they don't mind mashed potato and smells.

The National Health Surface was the invention of Doctor Beverage, the inventor of drinks, who later became Doctor Pepper, and he promised he would put everyone from a cradle into a grave. And that's a promise they keep to this day. Thanks to the NHS, you can just walk into your doctor's and get an appointment for any illness you're expecting to have in about two weeks.

And it's not just doctors. There are nurses, who are sort of miniature doctors. They look after less serious things, like children. And there are surgeons. Surgeons do years of training to learn which bits are which, how to take them out if that'll help and how to turn on taps with their elbows. Skills.

These days surgeons can get inside you using your keyhole, but in the olden days, even simple operations like sawing a lady in half used to be brutal, and the only way to make it more bearable was to put a bit of wood in someone's mouth to stop all the complaints coming out. But now we have anesthetic, which made the process easier because instead of blocking the mouth, it actually blocked the pain, using a bit of wood so tiny it could fit inside a needle. I mean, I assume it's still a bit of wood. Like a sort of wondersplinter.

Giving someone an anesthetic is a bit like putting a TV on standby. It's not on, but it's not off. There's not a little red light, instead the human body goes "ping...ping...ping..." so you know it's still working. That's when the surgeons can go in and try to remove bits of you without your nose buzzing.

Medicine and medical treatment have come a long way, baby. Only a few years ago, we thought chewing gum would turn into a tree in your stomach. Now, techniques like stem cell research mean that we're only decades away from building an entire person without having to wait nine months for a baby.

And, as we all get healthier, doctors will have less and less to do, and will die out like **dinosaurs**. Maybe one day the only way to see a doctor will be in a museum, and our children's children will ask us, "Granny, what was doctors?" And we'll say, "They were like shops where you could get free better." And they'll think we're delusional. Which we will be. Because grannies mainly are.

Unanswered Questions about Medicine

💀 Why aren't there more songs about doctors?

💀 Why can't you get medicine on crisps? That'd be much nicer.

💀 Can you fix people by turning them off and turning them on again?

Middle Ages

The Middle Ages came, as the name suggests, in the middle of time—just 4,539,998,400 years after the Earth was discovered and 1,600 years before now—which means we know the Earth will end in the year 4,539,999,400, which is handy for planning, although, as I found out during a very boring fortnight in Lowestoft, the calendar on my phone goes up to the year 292,471,210,647—and that's 288 billion years after the Earth ends. And probably, by then, we'll all living be on Mars. Or Bounty. Whatever's left, really.

KNIGHTS AND CASTLES

Just as the British people had revolved from primitive grunting cavemen to people wearing sacks and living in huts, in the Middle Ages they revolved again. This new SuperBrit wore metal clothes and lived in a giant fortified house. He was called a knight. And his home was called a castle.

In the time of knights, everything went totally Robocop. It was a bit like the difference between when policemen had soft jackets and jolly helmets and now, when they've got stab vests and semi-automatic submachine guns. This was known as the Age of Shivery, because it gets dead cold if you're only wearing tins.

Castles were built by kings. They were big, which made them posh, and hard to get into, which made them even posher, like fashion shows or restaurants where all the menus are in foreign and you have to talk quietly.

The knights' job was to defend the king. They were the olden days equivalent of those people with earpieces that hang around

VIPs. And a knight was expected to do his duty, which included championing good over evil, protecting the weak and being kind to women. Which is why Sir Jimmy Savile was never knighted.

MEDIEVAL ENTERTAINMENT

In the Middle Ages, the country was taken over yet again, but this time the invader was not a foreign army or a plague of mosquitoes: it was fun.

There hadn't been any fun in Britain before—just wars and stones and going to church. Suddenly, everyone was dressed as playing cards, and it was permanently like being at Glastonbury —with jugglers, jesters, a chill-out tent where you can play chess and something called minstrels, which wasn't chocolate buttons, but a sort of olden days Mumford and Sons, but worse.

This was the Age Of Entertainment. Suddenly there were songs you could sing along to, instead of just monks going ommmmm. There were plays, and games, and there were stories, too, instead of just the Bible.

Some of the best stories were written by a lecherous old cork called Geoffrey Chaucer. Although he might sound like a smelly maths teacher, Chaucer was the raciest writer of his day. His stories, like parks at night, are full of sex and poo.

The Canterbury Tales was Chaucer's attempt to do a *Confessions Of…* series: *Confessions Of A Knight, Confessions Of The Wife Of*

Bath and *The Confessions of General Prologue*. The bawdiest (which is posh code for "muckiest") of all was *The Miller's Tale*, in which a woman sticks her arse out of a window in the dark and a priest kisses it and then a man sticks his arse out of the window and farts in the priest's face, and he puts a red-hot rod up the bloke's brown eye. It's all so rude that it's written in a secret foreign language, so the police don't find out, with words like "whilom" and "yclept," which are probably anagrams of something so filthy it would make a sailor spit.

Chaucer's saucy stories started by being told out loud. Most people couldn't read, so they went round someone's house who knew some stories, or could read, like when people go to the pub to watch Sky Sports, because they can't read.

But *The Canterbury Tales* were so popular that they weren't left just as sound coming out of a peasant's horrible mouth: they were remastered in pin-sharp book format. **Books** weren't pointless like they are today. They were full of stuff for educated people, like BBC4 or museums. And, now Chaucer's smut was written down, other people could read it. Which probably made them wonder what the bloody world was coming to.

Most other popular pastimes were based on the madcap fun of cruelty. Public executions were popular—and they weren't just quick deaths like the electric chair (which was probably the acoustic chair back then)—they were long, complicated occasions that involved people being choked and having bits cut off or ripped out and dragging them around. It makes ISIS look like

Crowded House. There was also bear-baiting, shin-kicking and cockfighting—which isn't what it sounds like, even though I checked. Twice.

There were also lots of games invented we still play today, like Hazard, Alquerque and Knucklebones, none of which you've ever heard of.

Money

Money is at the heart of the UK economy, and many others. People fight for it, die for it and put it in china pigs. Money makes the world go round, thanks to that slot at the North Pole.

So what is money? Put simply, money is the best way we have of telling how much money you've got.

Over the centuries, lots of things have been used as money, including amber, wheat, eggs, travelers' checks, feathers, book vouchers, lobsters, beads, gold, leather, Nectar points, rice, peas, mugs and sheep. But carrying loads of sheep around in your pockets isn't easy, and olden days people didn't even have trousers, so you had to stuff the animals in your tights, which is why rich men like **Henry of Eight** stood with their legs so far apart.

Some people ask: Is money real? The answer might surprise you: Yes. I've got some ten pees in my purse, so I can prove it. On one side it's got a lady, to show it's money for humans, and on the other side it's got a lion in a crown, to remind people not to give money to animals, because they'll only spend it on stupid shit.

People get paid different amounts of money so they can buy the things they need. A cleaner doesn't get paid as much as a millionaire, because millionaires' stuff is much more expensive. So the system is rigorously fair.

Money started off as metal, then it was paper, but increasingly these days money isn't something you can hold in your hand or bite like a pirate: it's stored in the imagination of computers. You might think that means money's getting lighter, but if you carry a computer full of money in a shoulder bag, you know it's even heavier than coins. And there's another problem: it turns out computer money is vulnerable, which means it can easily be vulned. And that's bad news for ordinary people like you, and even me.

In the year 208, there was a global financial crunch, when it turned out the banks' computers had been lying about how much money they had. The clever solution to this was Quantity Deveasing or QE, which is where you make more money out of thin air. Air is a good thing to make money out of because everyone needs it to breathe, so it's more valuable than gold, which nobody needs.

All the money that disappeared in the crunch was only made up, so it's a shame that everyone had such a horrible time because of it. It's like going to prison for murdering your imaginary friend. But one thing leads to another. And—like that thing where a fish gets eaten by a bigger fish, which gets eaten by a really big fish—the financial crisis was very much a "fish's circle."

It may be that no one really knows what money is. It may always be an unsolvable problem, like a crossword or a Rubik's cube. Perhaps the only thing we really know for sure about money is that, without it, we'd all be a lot worse off.

Unanswered Questions about Money

🍦 When you put a coin in a chocolate machine, how does it get to the bank. Is there a tube?

🍦 Where is the money stored in a coin?

🍦 If I forgot my PIN number, could I split the card open with a knife and get the money out?

Mozart

Of all the composers who have ever lived, none has written quite as many tunes as Wolfgang Rock Me "Amadeus" Mozart.

Mozart was born in 1756 in Austria, though it wasn't called Austria then. By the age of three, he was playing the piano, though it wasn't called the piano then. People thought he was The Prodigy, but The Prodigy wouldn't be born for over 200 years, so he could go about his everyday composing business without people mistaking him for the angry one and asking him to play "Firestarter" on the harpsichord, which left him more time to invent hit songs like "The Marriage Of Fig Roll" and "Concerto No.21," which he did.

Little Tiny Mozart wrote his first tunes aged five, and his first symphony aged eight. This is amazing, because he could have been out on his bike or climbing a tree like a normal kid. His parents sent Mozart and his sister out on tour around Europe performing their hits before the courts of Prague, Vienna, Paris, Munich and London. Why they did their tunes in court is a mystery, but probably because there were judges there, and they were hoping to get through to the judges' houses, where they'd have a better chance of a record deal.

By the time Mozart wrote his first opera at the age of four-teen, it was clear he wasn't normal at all. For a start, he was fourteen and could sit through an opera. Something had to be done. So he got a job as an organist. But that didn't stop his compulsive tune-writing, and he just kept forcing more and more music out of himself, like he had the shits, but with notes.

Eventually, poor and exhausted, he took to his bed to die. Even then, he couldn't do it without music, so he wrote his most famous last work, the Requiem, which is a very long song in Latin about dying. It's very much the East 17's "Stay Another Day" of its day, and would have been on a John Lewis ad if Christmas had been invented back then. But he didn't finish it, and it died along with him in 1791. He was thirty-three, the same age as Guy Fawkes was when he died, leaving his greatest work—blowing up parliament—also unfinished.

Mystery of Life, The

Life is a mystery, if you believe the people who say that "life is a mystery." I don't. I think it's hundreds of bloody mysteries. There's so much we don't know. When is science going to stop mucking about with 5G and driverless **cars** and answer the really difficult questions?

Things like:

- Where does your lap go when you stand up?
- Is wind just angry air?
- What's the heaviest day of the week?
- What happens down holes?
- Is a computer actually a slave?
- Where do they hide the music in a piano?
- If I kept a monkey long enough, would it evolve into a boyfriend?

- Where do clouds go at night?
- What's the most political thing that's ever happened?
- Are busses ticklish?
- What's it like not to be here?
- Who discovered the one times table?
- Why don't boats go soft when they get wet, like biscuits do?
- Why are hot days blue, but hot taps red?
- How many places are there in the world?
- What is noise made of?
- Why is the word "big" small and the word "small" bigger?

Nanotechnology

Nanotechnology is the word for machines that are so small and fiddly that you can't even see them. Imagine the keyboard off a BlackBerry, but worse.

Nanotechnology is to normal technology what Miniature Heroes are to full-sized chocolate. Imagine a Miniature Heroes version of a lawnmower or a clock. Then forget that and think of something smaller. And then halve it. And imagine a magnifying glass, and imagine you're looking through it, and imagine you can't see anything. That.

Scientists say that if nanotechnology keeps advancing at the current rate, eventually we'll have machines so small that we won't be able to even use them or find them. Machines so small they could be injected up your arse, if that seemed like a good idea. People of the future might breathe nano-machines in, or fart a cloud of tiny, tiny, tiny lifts and jet skis and hairdryers.

When machines are that small, you have to ask what's the point. It's all very well having a bus the size of an ant, but people need to get smaller too or they'll just squash all the busses. The future, once again, hasn't been thought through. Nanotechnology needs nanopeople. But to those nanopeople, the nanotechnology just looks normal sized. So probably let's not bother.

Newspapers

Newspapers are a sort of paper version of Twitter for your nan. Apparently they still exist, but only outside petrol stations near the briquettes, behind little plastic windows, like a little news zoo.

Newspapers were how people in olden times found out what was going on the day before. The words in the newspaper would be made up by people called journalists. A "journalist" is what we nowadays call a "content provider," someone who copies and pastes what people are saying on Twitter and puts it into sentences, and it's those sentences that make Twitter into news. But in newspaper times, people in the news didn't just type up what they were thinking and doing, journalists had to actually go out and find out what was going on themselves, usually by hacking people's phone messages. It was a different world.

Newspapers had different sections you didn't want to read, like sport or overseas news, and stuff you did, like the word "jumble" and Fred Basset. You "scrolled" to the bit you wanted by putting the bits you didn't want in the bin, which is bad for the planet. Luckily now we can get exactly the parts of a newspaper that we want delivered straight to our phone, though it has made painting a shelf harder because you can't put the *Daily Mail* Sidebar Of Shame underneath to stop your table getting painty like you could with the family supplement. And it's impossible to start a fire using the Guardian app. Which is good for the planet too.

Some of the most famous newspapers such as *The Times* and *TV Quick* started in coffee shops in the 1800th century and by Victorian times they could be seen everywhere. Holding that day's newspaper was a sign that you were keeping up with events. Either that or you were helping your kidnapper prove to the police that you weren't dead yet.

Newspapers made ordinary people feel part of big events, whether it was the sinking of the *Titanic*, men pretending to land on the Moon, the death of Lady Diana or Kinga off *Big Brother* sticking a wine bottle up her growler. Without newspapers we would never have heard of Piers Morgan, Rupert Murdoch or Jeremy Clarkson, so it's understandable that in the 21st century the average person no longer buys a daily paper, in an attempt to stop it happening again.

Nightmares

Your brain is very much like a TV. During the day, you see all sorts of stuff that basically makes sense, even if a lot of it's boring: road signs, grass, the news. But then, just like TV, at night, all the weird stuff comes on: *Life Below Zero, The House Of Lords, Russell Howard Live.* This is called dreaming. And when it's a horror or something with subtitles, it's called a nightmare.

A basic nightmare involves running out of crisps. This has all the elements: primal panic, the possibility of starvation and monsters. A more sophisticated nightmare might be thinking you're being chased round a spooky old house by a six-headed giraffe that wants to know what 13 x 12 is. Or that you're the last sandwich in a Boots meal deal and you're headed for the compacter, except the compacter has the face of Radzi from *Blue Peter,* who should be a nice guy but is now a giant chewing shipping container that wants to eat you, and anyway you're a pathetic combination of tuna and cucumber and look how disappointing you are to one of the nicest people, who you've turned into a killing machine.

Some therapists like to analyze dreams, as if they could possibly mean anything.

.... 𝄞 ....

Oedipus Complex

This is an idea come up with by the psychopath Sigmund Freud to explain why men are mental and cross all the time, and won't calm down at traffic lights. His excuse was that when they were babies, all men wanted to kill their dad and do their mum. It's one of those excuses that doesn't really help, because that's worse than the thing it's explaining.

This complex is quite simple. It's named after the Greek character Oedipus. Oedipus murdered his dad and married his mum, by accident, which is how you can tell the difference between him and Bagpuss, who didn't.

Freud eventually realized his brilliant theory only explained men, and was therefore missing half of humans, so was about as useful as a theory that explains why everybody is Chinese. To make up for this, he invented an explanation for why women are mental, which he called penis envy. This was even worse than the Oedipus one, because it was based on the idea that women dig around in their pants at some point and get cross that someone's nicked their wanger. It's the sort of idea that tells you more about Freud than anybody else, but what can you expect from a man who wanted to hump his mum?

Olympics

The Olympics are an international sports contest that take place every time we have one. It's a chance for all nations to gather together and find out who's the best at running, jumping, throwing, horses and corruption.

In 2012, Britain won the Olympics for the first time in ages. It was a wonderful time, when the whole country came together, rich and poor, black and white, able-bodied and disabled, with a single aim: to boo George Osborne. It was bloody brilliant. I don't think we've been quite that happy since.

Some of the sports they do at the Olympics are sensible (running as fast as you can, getting rid of an unwanted hammer you can't be arsed to eBay) and some are stupid (horse disco, running as fast as you can but also a bit slowly at the same time, waving a ribbon in a foundation garment). The most important event is usually the competition to see who can run the fastest for not very long, because this is the only Olympic skill that has an everyday application, because of busses.

Every so often the Olympics is snowed in, but they do their best. That, for me, is the true Olympics Spirit.

P

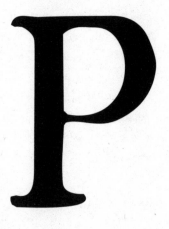

Pasta

In the olden days, there used to be two types of pasta: spaghetti and spaghetti hoops. Then a new pasta was discovered — tinned pillows called ravioli. Since then, science has had pasta breakthrough after pasta breakthrough, and loads of new pastas have been found.

There's lasagna, which is sort of postcards; there's farfalle, which is moths; there's rigatoni, which is sewers; there's conchiglie, which is fists; and, of course, there's alphabetti, which is a sort of spaghetti, but more alphabetty.

Who knows what future pastas will be discovered. Pasta that can be downloaded to your microwave without needing to open a tin. Hover-pasta, perhaps. Or pasta that can turn back time. Maybe a probe will discover pasta on Mars, the first alien pasta, and the world will come together in peace to welcome it at a ceremony where the cleverest person on Earth, maybe the ghost of Stephen Hawkings, or her who does the numbers on *Countdown*, gets to eat the Mars pasta and tell us what it tastes like. It would be beautiful. I, for one, can't wait. Pasta's brilliant.

Photocopiers

A photocopier is a machine that makes copies of flat things on paper. They used to have one in the office at my old school for doing forms for trips. Nobody knows how photocopiers work. Even the man who invented them, the Earl of Photocopier, didn't ever open one up to find out, for fear that it contained the devil.

Basically, you put the paper on the top that you want more of, and press the green button, then more comes out. Nobody knows where from.

Legend has it that people used to sit on photocopiers at office parties, but this doesn't make sense, because it's not like there aren't plenty of chairs in offices. Besides, you'd be up so high you'd be looking down at your manager's bald patch, which is a tough one to style out.

Nowadays everyone has a printer instead, which works by **computers**, so that makes some sort of sense. But photocopiers are basically magic, which is why they were got rid of, in case someone used one for evil, maybe photocopying Hitler.

······································ 🖰 ····································

Polarization

Magnets are proper fucking weird. They're either facing one way or the other. They're like the **Brexit** vote, but with somewhere to go, instead of nowhere to go and no idea of how to get there.

If you take two magnets and place their identical faces against each other, they'll try to hate each other, like two people of the same political or religious position do. But if you take two magnets and face their bums and mouths at each other, they'll try to cooperate, like a sort of scientific human centipede.

There's this theory that, if the magnetic poles of the Earth ever decide to change their minds, everything will go to shit. But it might be quite exciting. You'd have to hold maps upside down. Right-handed people would be the new minority. We'd have to rewire all our plugs—electricians would be millionaires overnight. There'd be T-shirts reading "East Is The New West." Maybe we'd have to drive on the wrong side of the road. Clocks might start running backward. Take that, boffins.

Pornography

A niche hobby, basically extreme people-watching, that used to be restricted to the top shelf of the newsagent, but which has really caught on and now forms about 110 percent of the internet.

Quorn

Once upon a time, no one needed to be vegetarian, because that would have been insane and you'd have been rightly chained to the wall of a very welcoming asylum for it. Then it became OK. And that's when the rot set in. Or, as it's now called, Quorn.

Quorn is what scientists call "matter," which is also what they call the stuff between your toes and the stuff that gets scraped out of U-bends and the gutter of the washing machine—basically, anything gray that isn't papier maché but looks and tastes a lot like it.

Yet Quorn, which is made out of recycled takeaways or something, is actually not bad. The **sausages** are quite good, even though they look like they're made of dead people's thumbs (though they can't be, because that wouldn't be vegetarian, even if the thumb owners were—actually, that's a problem, isn't it? Vegetarians are made of meat. How can someone made of meat be a vegetarian? Has anyone done this yet?)

Quorn does its best to look like food, even though it isn't. It assumes the form of sausages and burgers and mince, even though it's just matter. It's a bit like that bit in *Fantastic Beasts And Where To Find Them* where all the stuff assembles itself into the shape of an Obscurus. So, if you eat Quorn, you're eating an Obscurus, but with added salt, so it's OK.

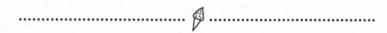

R

Radio For

Most radio is designed to attract minicab drivers, with its combination of catchy tunes from when the minicab driver was young and had anything at all to look forward to, blended with the sound of other minicab drivers calling in on their breaks to complain about how it's not like it was when they were younger and all this music was on.

But one radio station is different from all the others—Radio For. Radio For is short for Radio For Clever People. It's almost completely full of people talking, but not one of them is a mini-cab driver in a Morrison's car park. They're all full of facts and stuff they've read instead of just stuff they've heard on the radio from other minicab drivers.

The clever people on Radio For can tell you about gardening, politics, current affairs, history, what it's like to be stranded on an island with only music to eat, the weather if you're on a boat —you can even hear spy recordings of cow-owners having affairs near teapots in the countryside.

But it does show off. There's one program where people have to explain something in only sixty seconds without saying anything twice or repeating themselves. I can't remember what it's called. And another program where a really tetchy man called Mervyn or something is rude to people who are cleverer than him. He sounds like he's about to draw a sword, but he never does.

It's all very well being a radio station for clever people, run by clever people, but it's very alienating when there's no one on any of the programs who is normal. Maybe they should give someone like Paddy McGuinness a show where he just tries sandwiches while humming the charts or something. I'm just saying, it might make Radio For popular at last. Then it could be Radio For Everyone, or Radio For All Four Corners Of The Country, and change its name to reflect that, maybe, to something catchy, like Radio Four.

Roman Nempire, The

Some time in AD, the first tourists arrived in Britain. They came from Italy, but to preserve the element of surprise, they didn't call themselves Italians. They called themselves Romans.

The Romans were like the Britons, but from the future. They had roads and central heating and brooms on their heads. They took over the places they arrived in and made them all the same —something that wouldn't happen again until Pret A Manger. And they planned to make Britain a part of their big scheme, which they called The Roman Nempire.

The Roman Nempire was spreading all over the known world, which at the time was much smaller, because it was younger, like a kitten is smaller than a cat. The Romans were civilized, which meant that when a pile of people just started having sex, or eating so much that they threw up, they did it in Latin.

The Romans were so advanced they came with Latin pre-installed, like doctors or Boris Johnson. But unlike Boris Johnson they could speak in public, and use combs. They had a huge civilizing influence on primitive Brits, teaching us to wash and walk on our hind legs and to not just bite cows but to use a fork. They basically gentrified a primitive Britain. It was a bit like opening an artisan bakery in Hull.

The Romans also had a thing about straight lines: rows of soldiers, numbers, walls, mosaics (which are tiles you can almost be bothered to look at) and—most importantly—roads. Before roads was invented, you had to travel around by standing at the edge of your village wishing you could teleport or seeing how far you could jump.

But what the Romans really loved was bathing. Before them, water was just in the sky, as rain. Now they'd tamed it. Baths were places to meet people, to exchange gossip, to find stuff out, to get naked and show strangers your genitals. They were very much the internet of their day. And the Romans loved bathing so much they built a whole massive bathing complex and named the city after it: Bathe.

To an unsophisticated British tribesperson, all covered in mud with hair spiked up and a club, the baths at Bathe must have looked incomprehensible. It would be like Steve McFadden getting on board Concorde. He knows it's special. It's cleaner than anywhere he's ever been. It's exciting. *And he doesn't understand it.* He doesn't know how to behave. He might do a poo on the floor. Or start biting people, in panic. Maybe he'd smash it up to try and get to the magic inside. Or worship the people who made it, building a primitive shrine out of his shoes and howling.

Despite all this, some people resisted the Roman invasion. One was called Boadicea until recently, when she changed her name, like Prince used to, but while dead, which is frankly a bit late for a rebrand. Queen Boudicca came from Norfolk, like so many rebels —Myleene Klass, Ed Balls, Delia Smith—and she hated the Romans.

So she led a barbarian army in revolt and attacked Colchester, turning it from the bustling capital into a smoldering hellhole full of weeping and despair which you can still visit today.

Rome was the most advanced warfare machine on the planet. But Boudicca's army fought back with the weapon they knew best. Spikes. And lost. Because spikes.

Once Boudicca was crushed, the Romans ruled over Britain for years, until suddenly they had to rush home because they remembered they'd left a complete collapse of civilization on.

But their influence has never gone away. Imagine a Britain without wine, roads, Caffè Nero, baths, Cornettos, Aston Villa, aqueducts, alphabetti spaghetti, the Fiat Panda, the mustache, Milli Vanilli, paella, bukkake, hand gestures, the isosceles triangle, Viennetta, toga parties, pictures on floors and Cesar dog food. It's unthinkable. So to the Romans we have to say a great big Latin thank you: THANKVS YOV.

Rugby

Rugby is technically a sport, but only in the way that darts or hopping is.

What happens, as far as I can tell, is that two teams of different color men compete to get hold of a sort of giant eye. They throw the eye around and deliberately fall over with it, and sometimes they kick it over a big H. It's a sort of cross between *You've Been Framed* and *Sesame Street*.

But it's an affectionate game as well. The men all get together for great big group cuddles or lift each other up like they were going to do a piggy-back or lie on top of each other like at a pajama party. It's great to see men getting in touch with their feminine side like this. Rugby must be one of the most feminine sports there is.

Some of the men wear sort of bandages for fun, either on their heads or their legs—and their legs are fucking enormous. It's like someone built a load of Frankingsteins out of the rotating things in kebab shop windows.

Most rugby teams are named after animals, like Lions, Wallabies, Tigers, Springboks, Falcons and the Welsh, and they tend to come from cities, because there's more grass to play on there than there is in the countryside, which is mainly mud and rivers and tractors. There's even a city named after the sport—it's the city of Rugby.

There are two types of rugby—rugby league and rugby onion. One is faster and smaller than the other, and the other has a different name. Some players can do both, which is amazing. It's like when you found out Hugh Laurie could play the piano as well as being a doctor.

The biggest game of rugby in the world is The Six Nations, where six whole countries play against each other to find out which country is the best out of all the countries in the whole world, out of all the countries that give a shit about rugby, which is six. Usually this is played on the other side of the world, so the pubs can open early.

.... 📱 ....

Russian Revolution, The

Russia in the 1900th century was ruled by a king called the tsar, which is Russian for star, but they do all their letters backward, so it's easy to see what's happened there.

The king, Nicholas 11, was very, very rich, while everyone else in Russia mainly ate mud, mixed with vodka, to take away the taste of mud. One day some of Russia's top boffins decided this system was wrong. Until then, only France had noticed that kings have all the money even though they do arse-all. The idea of noticing this was so unusual that nobody here in Britain has ever thought it at all. The closest we came was asking the Queen to fix her own castle when it was burned down that time, and insisting on only giving her £18,000,000 toward the bill.

Sharing the **money** round so that everyone had sort of the same is called Communism, and it was invented by a man called Karl Marx. He wrote a book called *Das Kapital*, so called because he wrote it in London, a city which has a capital letter at the start of it. In his book he said that all the money in the country should be divided up between the workers and none of it given to the king, who wouldn't need it any more because he'd been shot.

It was a neat plan and really got people excited, so excited that one of Karl Marx's friends insisted that it was time for "power to the people"—and that man was John Lenin. Lenin led a revolution in 1917 that changed Russia from a corrupt country where a few people had uncontrolled power and riches into the country it is today.

The rest of the world was not keen on Russia's revolution and put up some ironed curtains, to show off the high standards of housekeeping in the free West. But Russia hit back by building nuclear rockets and making loads of posters of mums in head-scarves lifting tractors over their heads that you can buy in Camden Market now, and turning its women discus throwers into the Incredible Hulk. It was a war, but not a normal war, which is quite dramatic. This war was just low-level annoying instead, and went on for longer than anyone expected, like a cold, which is where it got its name. This was the cold war.

Sadly Communism was proved not to work in 1989 when a wall, built by Communist workers, fell down because Knight Rider had stood on it. When people saw how flimsy their walls were, nobody could take the Communists seriously. The work-ers had done a bad job, and standard practice with shoddy workmanship is to hold back payment, which the country did, stopping sharing the money between the workers, and giving it to people who could be trusted, who spent it on football teams and newspapers in other countries instead.

S

Sausages

Sausages are the only meat that can also be eaten by vegetarians. If you look in the supermarket, you will notice there is no vegetarian chicken or vegetarian beef, but there is vegetarian sausages. Vegetarians are happy to eat sausages, and in the case of Linda McCartney even lend her husband's name to them. Why? Because technically the sausage isn't an animal, because it cannot feel pain. This is why humans have for so long hunted and eaten the sausage. It's a guilt-free meat.

A sausage in a long bun is called a hot dog, because it looks like a dog (if you imagine a dog that lives in a long bun and has no legs or face). Other ways of eating the sausage include the casserole, the Wimpy bender-in-a-bun, and quickly.

In the wild, sausages are quite slow and easy to catch, using either a net, a gun, or a rod, if it's a freshwater sausage. Saltwater sausages are also popular, in tins. Even though the internet has changed the way we do everything, it hasn't affected the sausage at all. That's because it's impossible to make a sausage out of numbers, meaning that if there was a terrible nuclear pocalypse of some sort, and all the computers disappeared, we'd still have sausages, even though they'd be a bit burnt, which is bad news for anyone who usually leaves the black bits on the plate.

Senses

Humans can find out what's going on outside our heads by using our senses. Information comes into our bodies from outside and our brain analyzes the information and turns it into understanding, or, if we're hung over, it doesn't bother doing that and instead sets off a load of sirens and alarms in our head, to warn us that there is sunlight, and that bus is too red, and what are we meant to do about cups, until we go back to bed, often under our desk.

Some **animals** have senses we don't have, like bats have that sound thing that stops them bumping into caves, and cats have a way of reading your magazine by sitting on it and absorbing the best bits through their arsehole.

Without our senses, human beings would be no better than bollards.

There are, famously, eight senses. Here are seven of them.

1. Sight
Sight is what boffins call using your eyes. **Light** comes off things and goes into your eye through the black bit, which it turns out is a hole, even though I didn't want to know that because now I'm scared spiders might crawl into it while I'm asleep. It's handy that I'm the sort of person who sleeps with their eyes closed these days.

When light hits the back of the eye it makes pictures which the brain then tries to understand. If the picture is of something fairly simple—a flower or a lemon meringue pie or a hovercraft —the brain will say what it is quite quickly and move on. If it's something more complicated, like the instructions for assembling a sofa bed, or a film that's won a BAFTA in French, the brain will have trouble understanding it, and try to use other senses to help, like smell.

2. Smell
Dogs can smell loads better than humans, but only use it for evil, always sticking their nose in their groins and other dogs'

arses and piles of fox shit. Our human sense of smell is very limited by comparison, which makes it easier for us to live alongside dogs, who fucking stink.

Smell is done with the nose. Most senses require two of things—eyes, ears, hands. But we only have one nose. This is, again, to stop us smelling dogs so much, who stink.

We can tell when something is rotten using smell. Our other senses are not so finely tuned to detect rottenness, and we have to use other clues, like "Was it directed by Guy Ritchie?"

3. Taste

The other sense is taste. Taste is like smell for the mouth. We used to think that different parts of the tongue were used to detect different flavors, and Mrs. Mottishead made me draw a map of a tongue at school, but Wikipedia says that nobody thinks that any more, and it was a total waste of time, particularly all that coloring in. It's as bad as when they told us about man landing on the Moon, and that turned out to be made up as well.

When you think about a betrayal like the tongue map, it's hard to know who to believe any more, but a good answer would be "Not Mrs. Mottishead, because she's lying to you about tongues, and all that time you spent looking for a purple felt tip that hadn't dried out to color in your pointless lying tongue map could have been spent down Clinton Cards shoplifting Garfields," and the only sense I get from that isn't taste, it's regret. Bitter regret. A bitter regret which is tasted all over the tongue. Not just on the purple bit.

4. Feeling a bit sick

This is like a sixth sense, but it's the fourth sense on this list, because it's one of the most important. Feeling a bit sick is very highly developed in humans. Humans can feel a bit sick at a detail and depth that dogs and bats can only dream of. We have even invented corkscrew rollercoasters and Jagerbombs to explore the very limits of feeling a bit sick.

5. Touch

I forgot this one. It's done with the fingers, and is basically what they're for, that and pointing. Nerves send signals to the fingers to tell them to touch things. Then signals travel back up the nerves to tell the brain that the fingers have touched something, which the brain knew already because it sent the signal in the first place. It's like phoning your mum, and she keeps telling you stories that you told her yourself last week because she's run out of stuff to talk about.

6. Dread

The sense of dread is another one that humans do best. Dogs can't even dread at a thousandth of the strength as a human. They might have smell, but all their other senses are rubbish. If a dog had a proper sense of dread, it might anticipate how badly it would smell if it rolled in fox shit, and it wouldn't do it. Don't get me wrong, I like dogs, but they're a bit of a one-sense-wonder.

7. Sixth Sense

The sixth sense is the feeling you get that you can't explain that you might be a ghost, or that everyone else is a ghost, or that Bruce Willis is a ghost. Again, this is way more developed in humans than in any other animal, except hippos, who think about almost nothing else.

.... 🎞 ....

Shakespeare, William

Even though he's been dead for thousands of years, we still talk about William Shakespeare. But why? We don't talk about Les Dennis any more, and he's still alive, and he hasn't done anything wrong. Well, the answer is: because Shakespeare was the best at writing there has ever been, which means everyone who does words for a living, from Dan Brown to Tim Rice, owes him so extremely much.

It's often said that if Shakespeare were alive today he'd be sending his scripts to **television** and film companies, who wouldn't make them because they were so long and boring. But back in his day, Shakespeare's plays were as popular as bottled water is now.

EARLY YEARS

William Boris Shakespeare was born on 23 April 1564, which was a Thursday. Elizabethan England was nothing like today's Britain: there were no toilets and no Sainsbury's Locals. We don't know much about Shakespeare's childhood, except that he must have had one, otherwise he'd never have become a grown-up, like Bart Simpson hasn't yet.

Shakespeare's father was a tanner. Back in the 1564s, people didn't go on holiday to Faliraki, they went to the next field, and it was only explorers and birds that went abroad, so if you wanted a tan, you got it done locally.

As a baby, Shakespeare showed few signs of becoming the most significant figure in literary history, so nobody bothered noting down the details of his life.

We do know that Shakespeare went to school in Stratford and Avon, and probably had trouble fitting in, like a lot of kids do who move schools. He was probably one of them really clever kids who had glasses and weird shoes and picked his nose during P.E. As a boy, he would have looked much like boys today, but bald and with a ruff instead of an Angry Birds T-shirt. In those days, water was too awful to drink, so even kids drank beer. So everyone at school—the kids and the teachers—would have been drunk, which, if you think about it, sounds amazing. It's no wonder he never learned to spell.

Shakespeare would never have had a bike or a Swingball or even a Furby, so he probably spent all his time making up stories. It's surprising there weren't millions of brilliant writers then. They had bugger all else to do. He might have written all sorts of stuff when he was at school, like "What I did on my holidays" or "The Tragedy of Father Christmas Part 1," which would be worth a fortune these days if only his stupid teachers hadn't chucked them in the bin.

He would have sung lots of nonsense playground rhymes, like "Mary, Mary, Quite Contrary" and "Ring O'Roses," which people say is about the plague, when it's obviously about hayfever—but he probably made some up himself, like "My Friend Billy Had A Ten Foot Willy." Bet you that's one of his. It's got a proper story, and a tragic hero.

One thing we know for sure about school in Shakespeare's time is that it was far easier than now, because you didn't have to study Shakespeare.

LOST YEARS

Between the age of eight and eighteen, we know nothing about what he was doing. There's a whole decade of his life unaccounted for, like Harold Bishop off of *Neighbors.*

There are several possibilities. He might have gone on a long gap year to somewhere exotic like Didcot Parkway. He could have gone time traveling into the future to see what a robot

Shakespeare would sound like. Or maybe he went like one of them weird people that disappears and turns up years later living in a caravan on a farm.

Anyway, the point is he went missing for a few years, like Peter Andre. And we can't explain it, like Peter Andre—because the records are simply not good enough, like Peter Andre.

SHAKESPEARE IN LOVE

At the age of when he was eighteen, Shakespeare married his teenage sweetheart, the actress Ann Hathaway. Because he was in showbiz, Shakespeare was always changing his name, like Cheryl Tweedy Fernandez, and his marriage certificate is in the name of William Shagspere, which is probably one of his rude jokes.

Being in love was a big thing for Shakespeare—you can tell because much, much later he wrote a film about it, and called it *Shakespeare In Love,* so we'd know. He also did what a slightly sappy boy does when he fancies a girl: wrote poems. Specifically, he wrote sonnets, which are a type of poem with an almost musical flow. Sort of like rap but designed especially to be impossible to dance to or enjoy.

But poems don't make much **money**. Only one person has ever made their fortune from poems—the poet Sir Clinton Cards, whose works still sell today, making him the world's first and only poetry magnate, apart from those packs of little words you get to put on your fridge.

Shakespeare needed money to support his wife and three children, and nobody wanted to pay for sonnets, because they were awful. So he converted sonnets into something that could make money: a play.

OLDEN DAYS THEATER

To the Elizabethan audience, a play was a sort of film, but one you couldn't pause unless you knew everyone in the cast and had a very loud voice.

Shakespeare's first play was *The Comedy Of Errors,* and it's obvious that he had trouble coming up with the characters, because he wrote a pair of twins as the lead roles, and then wrote another pair as well, which is basically cheating. His first play did well, but if Shakespeare wanted to make a go of it in theater, he couldn't do it in Stratford, or even Avon. He was going to have to go where it was all at: London.

People in London only really liked beer and shouting and public hangings, so anything arty wasn't allowed in the main bit and had to go and live on the south side of the river, where rich people never went, just like nowadays. But pretty much as soon as Shakespeare arrived, there was an outbreak of bionic plague. There's no evidence that it was Shakespeare's fault, but you never know. He was a man capable of more things than most men.

The bionic plague killed about 10,000 people in London, and when the ones who were left had finished coughing, they needed cheering up, so the theaters re-opened. And they needed stuff to show in them, otherwise they'd just be buildings full of people staring in total bewilderment at just walls.

It's hard to believe today, but back then people really did go to the theater on purpose. It was one of the few things they could do when they weren't busy working or coughing. There was no TV or cat videos, so for entertainment, people would mainly look at the sky. But with no planes, there was nothing really on the sky, so theater became really popular (most theaters left their roofs offs, so if you preferred, you didn't have to join in, you could sit and watch sky instead, just like in pubs today). This was Shakespeare's moment.

SHAKESPEARE'S PLAYS

There was no doubt that Shakespeare was the best playwriter there had ever been. But there was enough doubt that he had to start his own theater company to put them on—like forming his own band, except they didn't have songs, they had long scenes where people said "zwounds" and "forsooth"—and they didn't have guitars, they had mustaches.

In many ways, Shakespeare was a DIY pioneer: not only did he write his own plays, and form his own theater company, but he even built a theater for all the above to go in. That theater was the theater called the Globe Theatre, and it still stands today, despite having been destroyed by fire over 400 years ago.

Here, he put on play after play—*Romeo And Juliet,* which is about a war between some sort of Kardashians and some sort of Baldwins; *Macbeth,* which is a play about Macbeth, whose name (Macbeth) you shouldn't say in a theater, even though it says Macbeth's name in the script and people call him Macbeth in the play and it says Macbeth on the posters; *The Tempest,* which is sort of like *Lost* except there's a wizard on the island—the nearest Shakespeare ever came to writing a proper Super Nintendo game; *Richard III,* which is about a sort of elephant man who'd give anything for a horse; *King Lear,* the really complicated one where someone loses an eye, like a boring Thor; and *A Midsummer Night's Dream,* his sort of Disney one, with all woodland animals and fairies and songs and that.

If you couldn't afford a seat at the Globe Theatre, you stood down the bottom with all the sweaty people to watch the show. (A bit like on trains now, except you *have* to be able to afford a seat just to stand with all the sweaty people.) The people standing down the bottom were called "groundlings" or "stinkards," because they stank and lingered on the ground. Some of them went to the theater just to sniff each other, because when you're poor you'll do anything for entertainment, like when old people take out their teeth to make kids laugh.

Shakespeare's plays used to be put on in the afternoon, while it was still light, so people used to skive off work to come to the theater. Except for the rich ones, who probably just told their secretaries to say they were in a meeting while, in fact, they were at the theater, watching people pretend to be royal and cross.

Because there was no roof, if it was raining at The Globe, you'd get wet, which is a pain—but if it was *meant* to be raining in the play, you'd probably think it was amazing because the weather was acting as well as the people on stage. There was also no microphones at The Globe, so the actors had to shout. Plays shouting isn't like proper shouting, like when a bus won't let you on: plays shouting isn't because of emotion, it's because they put the seats too far away. This can actually make going to see a play quite exciting, because of the fear that the people in the story will stop shouting at each other, and shout at you if you try to leave.

THE GOOD YEARS

Shakespeare was doing well. We don't have exact figures, but his spending would suggest he was earning a shitload. Which, in today's money, is an absolute shitload.

Shakespeare was the most famous person of his times except for Her Royal Majesty Queen Elizabeth The First, and Wet Paddy, this bloke who used to bite the heads off cats at the Southwark cockpit.

After he'd become rich and famous, Shakespeare bought loads of property and built a second theater. He was in many ways the **Donald Trump** of his day, except he had loads of talent and hadn't completely publicly lost his fucking Maltesers.

THE FINAL YEARS

We sometimes think of Shakespeare's later years as his dark years. But all his years were dark, technically, because the light-bulb didn't exist until Thomas Eddington discovered it in California, during the Queen Victorian era. It's amazing to think that when Shakespeare had the idea for *Hamlet*, a little candle would have appeared over his head. Really dangerous. Maybe that's what burned off the top of his hair.

At the end of his life, Shakespeare ran out of new ideas, and died. Which is something that had been done loads before. We don't know what Shakespeare's last words were. Probably ones he made up. But they never caught on.

Shakespeare died on his birthday, so it's impossible to know how old he was, because it might have been before or after the bit when your mum says, "You're not actually thirty until ten minutes past ten." So he could have been fifty-two or fifty-one. But dying on your birthday is a pisser for your family, who have to eat birthday cake with all tears in their eyes. And in that respect, Shakespeare's death was a tragedy—which is probably what he would have wanted.

So, we don't know when Shakespeare was born, what he did for ten years of his life, how he spelled his name, who wrote his plays, how old he was when he died or why he left his wife nothing but an all-right sort of bed in his will. We don't even know if he called himself Will or Bill or Willie or Billy or Wills or Shakey. But that doesn't stop whatever-his-name-was being the most talked about playwriter in all history, and some of it was quite a while ago, before even loom bands and Angry Birds.

But will there ever be another Shakespeare? I don't think so. Not exactly the same. Not these days. You can't get the ruffs.

Sir George

Sir George is the patron saint of old England. Scotland, Ireland and Walesland have their own ones, just like they get different ITVs.

Sir George, who was a Roman soldier born to Greek parents in either Turkey or what was then Syria but is now Israel, is the quintessential Englishman. He's also the patron saint of Aragon, Catalonia, Georgia, Gozo, Malta, Portugal, Romania and skin diseases, which makes him very important to you if you're on holiday or itchy.

Like Elvis, Sir George never came to England and like Elvis, he had a horrible death. Although being stretched, burned, poisoned, having molten lead poured in your eyes and mouth and sixty nails driven into your skull before being dragged through the streets and beheaded is still more dignified than dying by falling off a toilet.

It's probably a good thing Sir George never came here, because someone arriving from Syria, tooled up and ready to fight for an imaginary cause, sets off all sorts of alarm bells.

Some of the facts about Sir George are unclear, but one thing we do know for sure is that he slayed a mighty dragon. We don't know when, but we know it happened because a bystander took a painting of the event. It's one of the few facts to come out of the **Dark Ages**.

Thanks to Sir George there are no dragons in England any more. Presumably, they all moved to Wales, where they love them and put them on their flag. Sir George rid England so thoroughly of dragons that if you look for any evidence of dragons existing, you can't find any at all. To the casual viewer, it would seem that the dragon was never there, Sir George never killed it, and that the whole myth was nothing but a myth. But luckily for England's national identity, the myth of the myth being nothing but a myth is nothing but a myth.

We still celebrate Sir George's Day every April by dressing in T-shirts with the English rose on and wearing novelty hats in the shape of pints of lager and singing traditional English songs like "Tubthumping" by Chumbawumba.

And we still celebrate dragons today by sending everyone in Britain, one by one, to help be in *Games Of Throne*.

Skellingtons

Inside everybody is another, scarier version of them, made out of bones. This is called the skellington and is what stops a human from being like a bean bag or Morph.

A human skellington is made up of over 200 separate bones, but not so separate that they fall into bits. The knee bone's connected to the thigh bone. The thigh bone's connected to the hip bone. The hip bone's connected to the back bone. Most of this is explained in a song which doctors spend up to seven years studying before they are allowed to run an accident and emergency department.

Your bones keep growing until you are in your early twenties, when other stuff starts growing instead like your arse, beer gut and nose hair.

Bones are a good way to protect the sensitive soft parts of the body. For example, your brain is valuable—your body might need to use it at a moment's notice one day—so it is protected by a hard, thick skull. But some important parts have no protective bone covering, such as the tits and cobblers, even though being punched in them is bloody agony. **Evolution** sometimes lets us down. Maybe if we carry on punching people hard in the groin and chest as a way of winning fights quickly, then our children's children's children will have evolved tough little helmets over their knockers and knackers. That's if children don't stop happening because all the men's plums have been punched useless.

Some parts of the body are not visible on a skellington because they have no bones, like the elephant's trunk, which appears on skellingtons as a big hole. I bet Michael Jackson was gutted when he bought the Elephant Man's skellington and the best bit was missing.

When skellingtons do a dance, you can hear xylophones. Scientists still don't know why.

Soup

Soup is like food except it's a drink. Except it's not, it's a food. Get your head round that if you can.

If you want some food but also want a drink, it's basically perfect. Soup's been around for ages, and was how primitive humans managed to do food and drink in one before the evolution of the Wetherspoons meal and a pint deal.

The best soup is tomato, from a tin, off your lap with a cold. And the worst is oxtail, which is like evil Bovril. Other soups include carrots. This is the only thing that soup has in common with snowmen. Until some bright spark puts twigs in a soup, which is bound to happen at some weird restaurant one day.

Why do we even have weird restaurants? Nobody asked for weird restaurants. Just like nobody asked for driverless cars.

Anyway, that's soup.

Spotify

It used to cost **money** to buy music: you had to go down John Menzies to the tapes bit, ask for the latest UB40 or whatever and pay actual money. Spotify cuts out all that. Which is a shame because sometimes at the counter at John Menzies you could buy a bag of Ringos, and Spotify won't let you download crisps, even if you sign up for the Premium account.

Music is actually quite heavy—because the money it costs to pay the artists properly is heavy, because of coins. By not paying for it—either you or the people in the bands—everything can be lighter. So light that music can travel down an internet in a way that would be unthinkable to music lovers of the past, like that dog with the trumpet that was on carrier bags.

When records used to be in those bags, music was really heavy. Even the music that wasn't heavy, like light music, was heavy. And heavy metal was unbearable. I think the future's amazing. And that can only mean good things for UB40.

I've gone off music.

Stones Age, The

In the Stones Age, all people were cavemen. Cavemen were hairy, angry people who lived outdoors, like Bill Oddie.

Where modern day us is interested in shoes and NutriBullets and tennis, Stones Age man was mainly interested in stones. He used them to make basic weapons and tools, like hand axes. They're boring and shit by today's standards, but back then they were cutting edge, because they had a cutting edge. It was all pointy stones, pointy sticks, spikes. For people obsessed with pointy things they were pretty pointless.

Stones Age men were simple hunter gatherers. They'd hunt for big dinosaur steaks, and gather them into their primitive **cars,** with their feet poking out the bottom. And take them back home, where they'd put the saber tooth tiger out and pop a record on the pterodactyl record player. Then they would sit around the fire, which was the only thing they invented that wasn't made of stones, and tell each other stories—about stones.

French cavemen would paint pictures on the wall of their caves, but there's no evidence that British cavemen even put some shit on a stick and drew rude mammoths. They were bone idle. Even though there were other things just lying around, near the stones, like wood, and wool, they never bothered doing any drawing.

It would be easy to understand how amazingly lazy cavemen were if they had something nice to lie down on like a sofa or a cushion, but they only had stones. You'd think that would have given them some get up and go.

But no, they just collected stones.

Think how advanced we could be now if Stones Age man had only been arsed. We could have pretended to land on the Moon thousands of years ago. We could have been pretending to be on Neptune by now. And if Stones Age man had actually landed on the Moon, he'd have done exactly what we did—brought back stones.

Stones Age man needed big thrills, though, and got it in the form of Stonehenge. Cavemen had small stones. Now they could go and look at big ones. To Stones Age man, Stonehenge was a cross between Nemesis at Alton Towers—in that it was a spectacular attraction—and the queue for Nemesis at Alton Towers —in that it never fucking moves.

But these small, hairy creatures—sort of giants but normal size—spent generations sharpening stones and not inventing the razor, and hitting things together like cross chimps. As a result, Stones Age man left us a legacy of stones. He was basically an idiot. It's a wonder any of us is here.

Unanswered Questions about The Stones Age

🦻 Why was Stones Age man so stupid?

🦻 Why is there just spikes in museums, not the rest of their stuff?

🦻 Didn't they notice wood?

🦻 How did Fred Flintstone die?

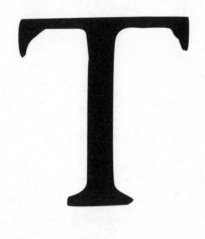

Taj Mahal, The

The Taj Mahal is one of the most spectacular buildings in the world, and one of the few to be made entirely of **ice cream**. (At least, that's how it looks.)

To stop it melting in the hot sun of India, where it lives, the builders must have used the same technology they use to make Baked Alaska. It is, by volume, by far the largest Baked Alaska on Earth. It was built in the 1600s to please the wife of the Indian king, who must have really liked ice cream, but was sadly too dead to enjoy it, and was instead buried, in chocolate sprinkles, at its heart.

That's if it's made of ice cream. The publishers refused to fly me there to run a taste test.

································ ································

Television

Once upon a time, you had to have a TV to watch TV. Now you don't need a TV at all. You can watch TV on your computer, your tablet, your phone and probably, by the time this book comes out, your toothbrush or your shoes. There'll probably even be a way of watching television in a book, by turning the pictures and sounds in the program into words and then putting a picture of someone from the program on the front so you don't mistake it for a real book.

The best new place for television is the television in your pocket: your phone. The phone used to be a thing for communicating with people. Now it's for looking at and ignoring people. Which is much more useful. Now you can watch *Loose Women* on the train and *Homes Under The Hammer* in the toilets when you're getting bored down the pub.

These days, the big screen in your front room looks a bit of a **dinosaur**. If there was a dinosaur with a big square face.

So what's better? Phone or TV?

TV has some of the most amazing wildlife programs on it, like *Blue Planet* and *Raa Raa The Noisy Lion*. But my old Nokia had Snake on it, which is not just wildlife, but also a game. So that's 1–0 to phones. TV's got loads of great game shows on it. But not Soda Candy Crush. Which is brilliant. 2–0 to phones. When you get bored with the TV or the adverts come on, where do you look? Your phone. 3–0 to phones. You can't take your TV into the bathroom with you to whack off to porn. 4–0 to phones. Unless you're P Diddy and you've got a TV already in your bathroom. And I'm not P Diddy. I'm P Cunk. So that's 5–0 to phones. My mate Nev's got a huge telly, like the size of a shop. But so what? I can hold my phone really close to my face and get the same effect. 6–0 to phones.

So our phones are basically TVs now, as well as phones and maps and computers and cameras and calendars and watches and calculators and weather forecasters and credit cards and them little minicab offices you get in Chicken Cottage.

And our TVs are basically giant phones that only do one thing. They're big, they're expensive if you don't get a twocked one from Smack Converters and—unbelievably—most of the time they're still in black and white, when they're turned off. My iPhone 5C's bright yellow, even when it's run out of battery. It's a joke.

Think of something you do every day, like ordering pizza. You just go on your Domino's app, order a large Meatzza Pizza with a Barbecue Stuffed Crust, and half an hour later Omar drives it round on a hot moped. If I wanted to order a pizza using my TV, I'd have to actually go on TV and persuade the producers to let me say, "If there's anyone from Domino's in Derby Street watching, could you send a large Meatzza Pizza with a Barbecue Stuffed Crust to my flat for about 8 p.m. as usual? Omar knows where I live."

And what if nobody was watching because they were busy making pizzas? What if my bit got edited out? People could *starve*. Which is why more people use phones than TV: because phones save lives.

Scientists predict that one day we'll all be doing everything on our phones, a bit like we already are.

Of course, the nightmare scenario—now phones are basically getting bigger and bigger again, after they spent years getting smaller —is that they'll become the size of TVs, and we'll all basically be carrying TVs round with us everywhere, like we're looters in a riot.

And then we'll have drunk people leaving their TVs on the train, people dropping TVs down toilets and having to put them in sacks of rice overnight, and everyone will have to have enormous pockets and giant handbags. And if that happens, we'll probably all start to evolve bigger fingers, and in a few generations' time, our grandchildren will be these gorgeous little kids with massive, fat hands, like the mascots at Disney or Miley Cyrus. And then we'll have to introduce giant cashpoints and extra large spoons and PlayStation controllers the size of tables and people who want to clap will probably have to wear ear protectors by law. If you think about it, it doesn't bear thinking about.

I wish they'd never made TVs and phones the same thing. I think it was a mistake. One of those things humanity is one day going to regret. Like walking upright. And yogurt.

By the way, "TV" is short for television. I should have said that up the top. But it's still true down here.

························ 🌍 ························

Time

As the world spins faster and faster, time seems more precious every day. But time is not like other precious things: you can't hold it, like a necklace, or taste it, like **money**. Yet some people say time is money. Which it isn't, or coins would tick. And you'd be able to spend it on stuff or put it in the bank or blow it on something daft. And who's ever heard of anyone spending time or saving time or wasting time?

So how many of us actually understand time?

Time has been around since before the beginning of time. Today, it's all around us—on our phones, in the corner of the news —but once upon a time, if you wanted the time, you had to make a special visit to the headquarters of time: Greenwich Clock Museum in Greenwich in London, the place where all time is made. All the clocks in the world are set from Greenwich, which must take ages. And when they say "the clocks go back" this is where they go back to, to have the new times put on. It's usually an hour.

So what is clocks?

Clocks was invented by the ancient Mesopotamians in ancient Mesopotamian times—but they didn't know they were ancient Mesopotamian times because there were no clocks to tell them what the times was.

Because of the shape of clocks, you might think that time goes in a circle. But it doesn't. It actually goes in a line. At Greenwich Clock Museum they've got the line it goes in: the famous Greenwich Marillion Line, made of heavy metal and named after the band Marillion, who are named after the Line. Every day that's ever happened starts at the Line. On one side of it is the past—and on the other is the future. So you can stand with your legs either side of it, and feel the present literally forcing itself cheerfully between your legs.

But even boffins who understand time don't understand what it is. Is it a physical thing? Is it alive? If it is alive, is it OK?

It's no wonder no one can explain time. When you start finding out about it, as I was made to, it gets insanely complicated. For instance, because of the speed of light, which is the fastest speed there is, the faster you're going, the longer time takes. So if you put a candle on a skateboard, and it's sitting still, the light's taking however long—but if you move the skateboard, the light's taking the same time, but the time is taking longer. (I think that's it.)

That must be why time flies when you're having fun, but when you're panicking or nervous, like when you're on an escalator and you realize you're standing still but still moving, you sort of freeze, and time stands still, like in *The Matrix.*

Perhaps the only thing we know for sure about time is that it's slowly running out for all of us. And that's a comforting thought.

················· 🌎 ·····························

Top Gear

The BBC loves making old programs again with different people in: they did *Porridge*, they did *Open All Hours* and they did *Are You Being Served?* But their most successful one was the reboot they did of *Last Of The Summer Wine,* where they took the three old men going downhill in an unlikely vehicle and gave it a complete makeover, adding loads of pizzazz and whizz-bang and changing its name to *Top Gear.*

Foggy, the tetchy, arrogant one, became the comedy character Jeremy Clarkson; Clegg, the quietly spoken one, became the character James May; and Compo, the scruffy little mischievous one, became the character Richard Hammond. And instead of confining their escapades to Yorkshire, the three of them capered around the world, hilariously crashing **cars** and ruining caravans and damaging the **environment** and slagging off foreigners and using all sorts of **language** and causing near-diplomatic incidents with the Argentinians, the Germans, the Mexicans, the homosexuals and the Romanians.

But much of the original *Last Of The Summer Wine* format remained: it was still three lovable old men wasting their time because they all had some fundamental personality flaws, and it was still watched by millions of slightly undemanding people week in and week out, long after it was past its best.

In the explosive final series, the character of Jeremy Clarkson lost his shit with a producer and walloped him for not being able to find a steak in a pub—which some people thought was going too far, and the show was cancelled.

Shortly after that, a spin-off show was launched—confusingly, also called *Top Gear*—starring Joey from *Friends* and the hilarious Chris Evans off of *TFI Friday*. They had a buddy-buddy relationship, like Butch Crassidy and The Sunny Delight Kid. But viewers didn't take to the pair, especially the Chris Evans character, a sort of millionaire schoolboy who'd won a competition, and he was eventually written out.

I don't know if it's still on. I only really watch *Love Island*.

Triangles

A triangle is any shape with three sides, except a coin, which has a head side, a tail side and a round-the-edge side but is apparently not a triangle.

The triangle is the only shape named after a musical instrument, except the symbol. Though one day the French will probably call a rectangle *"le synthesizer,"* maybe as a mark of honor when Daft Punk die. They're like that, the French.

The word "triangle" in English comes from the word "angle," meaning angle, and the word "tri," meaning three, because there are 180 angles in a triangle, and 180 divided by 10 is 18; and 18 is 3 times 6; and 6 is 3 times 2; and 2 is the smallest number, so therefore: "three-angles" = triangle: 180 angles.

The amazing thing about a triangle is you can fit those 180 angles into the triangle no matter how small the triangle is. Think of the tiniest triangle you can imagine (the one you fold a crisp packet into, or the top of a pencil, or the pointy hat on a microscopic wizard) and you can still fit every one of those 180 angles into it. They must be really squashed up.

Because of this, we can do some amazing calculations, knowing what we know about triangles. Hold onto your hats, especially if you're a microscopic wizard.

Each corner of a triangle has 60 angles in it (180 divided by 3), so that means there are 900 angles *outside* the triangle. These 900 angles outside the triangle are the angles you can't see, but you know are there. This is called dark maths.

That means there is a total of only 1080 angles in the entire universe: 180 inside the triangle, and 900 outside, everywhere else in the whole of everywhere. Those 900 angles are divided amongst all the triangles in the universe. And because there are

180 angles in each triangle, we can use this to work out how many triangles there are in the whole of space: 900 divided by 180, which makes five.

Proving that there are five triangles in the universe. We already know about the crisp packet, the pencil top and the little wizard. That leaves two more. One day, science may find the other ones, but they're probably on the other side of space.

·· 🌍 ··

Trump, Donald

See **Lies**.

·· 🌍 ··

Truth

These days it's hard to know what's true and what isn't. On the big issues, nobody can agree what's actually going on. Whether it's **Brexit**, or Trump, or the Loch Ness monster, we might as well all live on different planets. But outside our sexual media echo chambers is there anything we can all agree is true?

What is truth? The dictionary says it's a noun, whatever that is. But is that true? Can we trust the dictionary? Well, if you look up "dictionary" in the dictionary, what does it say? "Noun."

Again. Whatever that is. It's as if someone doesn't want us to know the truth.

Truth is what's actually happening. So it's true that I'm dictating this into my **iPhone**. And it's true that I've got some of the granola bar I had for breakfast stuck in my teeth. But the fact that my Nissan Micra turns into a pumpkin at midnight isn't true. So it isn't a fact. That was a trick. And you fell for it, Siri.

Some people say truth is stranger than fiction. That means it's stranger than that book where children are tortured by an army of orange dwarfs in a sociopath's chocolate factory, so you'll understand why nobody believes in it any more, because that's pretty fucking strange.

Scientists use something called proof to test if something is true. That means doing an experiment and always getting the same result. So if I toss a coin and always get heads, that would prove the coin was true. But if I got tails, even once, the coin would no longer exist. Which is why science is so expensive.

TRUTH AND FULLOSOPHY

Throughout history people called fullosophers have wondered if anything was true, and refused to accept reality, which was a good way to avoid having to get a proper job.

Aristotle said, "To say of what *is* that it is *not*, or of what is *not* that it *is*, is false. While to say of what *is* that it *is*, and of what is *not* that it is *not*, is true." To this day, nobody knows what he was drinking.

A fullosopher called Russell Bertrand, in many ways the Russell Brand of his day, said that many different ways of seeing the world might exist, but only one could actually be true, like how all the cakes in *Bake Off* look nice, but only one can win.

In the olden fashioned times, people didn't believe something was true because it was true but because someone *said* it was true, usually a priest or a god or anyone with a beard. Nowadays, we don't do that, because of Noel Edmonds. But some people think that belief is the same as truth. They say they believe in God, so there is a God. Other people say they don't believe in God, so there is no God. But nobody knows how needy God is—He might need to be believed in just to exist, like David Gest did.

In the 20th century, people started to mess around with ideas. Picasso painted pictures of impossible people with triangle faces and eyes on different floors—and as a result, someone I haven't found the name of came up with the idea of relativism.

Relativism has nothing to do with having your family over at Christmas—it's about saying that everything's up for argument, which is actually a *lot* like having your family over at Christmas.

Relativism is useful when there's no scientific proof that something is true. For instance, there's no proof that Bombay Bad Boy is the best flavor of Pot Noodle, even though everybody knows it is. So we just have to say that it's better than all the others. Especially Sticky Rib.

THE TRUTH ABOUT THE TRUTH

Spandau Ballet sang a song that went, "This much is true." What they meant is still hotly debated to this day, but the single cost about £1.10 when I bought it in Boots. That much was true.

It's hard to know what's true and what's not when even clever people like Stephen Fry used to be on the television all the time saying there's no such thing as the Moon just to piss off Jonathan Creek. Are these trees real? Are those trees real? What about love? Or Yorkshire pudding?

What about me? How do I know if I'm real? For all I know, I might have been made up by someone for a laugh.

Unanswered Questions about Truth

🗑 If someone says, "Hello, I'm a liar," how do you know they're telling the truth?

🗑 Can you tell if someone's telling a lie if they do a blowoff when they're saying it?

🗑 Do old people eat talcum powder?

🗑 Is there really a truth fairy?

🗑 If you swallow bubble gum does an apple tree grow in your stomach?

🗑 If you turn a lie detector upside down, does it become a truth detector?

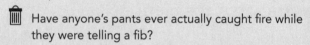 Have anyone's pants ever actually caught fire while they were telling a fib?

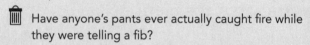 Is it true what Einstein said—that if you were traveling at the speed of light, and you turned the lights off, you'd crash into something?

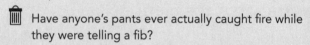 Is the sky actually blue or is it another color and we can't see it, because there's all that blue in the way? Like the green bottle they put Appletiser in.

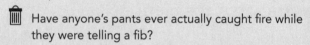 When someone does an E and tells you you're their best mate—is that them lying or telling the truth?

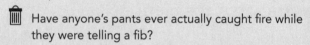 Where does the truth go when it dies? (I got this question from the words of a power ballad.)

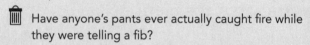 Has anyone ever photographed a truth?

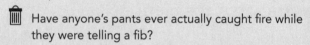 In court, when you promise to tell the whole truth and all that, why do judges still dress like twats and nobody says?

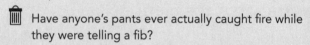 Is a white lie racist?

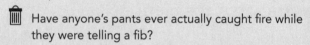 In that Ricky Gervais film, *The Invention Of Lying*, why was it ever made?

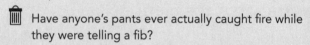 If you took a lie detector out into a field, could it find where people *say* gold's buried but isn't?

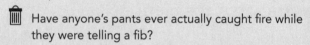 If truth is measured in yeses, is that why there's YESterday but NO tomorrow?

United States of Americans, The

The United States of Americans is a great big country on the other side of the world (or "the pond," as they sometimes call it) where there's Hollywood and hot dogs and huge **cars** and guns everywhere and cowboys and cactuses and skyscrapers and superheroes and stars and stripes.

But there's more to the USA than that. Although, to be fair, not much more. That's quite a lot already.

THE CONSTITUTION

In Britain we have never needed a written-down thing that tells us what our country is, because we just do whatever the Queen says or she cuts our head off, but in America, they have a book called the constitution, to tell them how to be American.

The American constitution is like the most important thing for Americans, because it goes back so far into history. It was written down in 1787, making America nearly as old as Addis, the company that makes pedal bins and washing up bowls.

The U.S. constitution is like the instructions for America. Every country needs rules, especially a new country like America, which had only been invented a few years before, after being taken from the people who lived there before. They hadn't had any instructions at all except the ones about putting up wigwams, and look where it got them.

To make America work only required seven very basic things to be written down. This told everyone what America was, so everyone agreed, and stopped there being a war about it, except the one that started almost immediately a few years later.

Writing those seven things onto paper literally set them in stone so they can never be changed—plus twenty-seven changes that have been made to those seven things—or there'll be a war.

The changes are called Amendments, because you say "Amen" after them, and the one you hear most about is the Second Amendment. This is the one that says all Americans have to carry at least one gun, and fire it into the air if a stranger comes into the saloon. Another amendment to this amendment was invented by the monkey-fighting actor Charlston Heston who decided that if the **government** wants to take a gun away from an American citizen, they have to give him some cold dead hams as a prize.

WHAT AMERICANS MEAN WHEN THEY SAY THINGS

In America, they speak English except they change loads of the words, so you have to sort of struggle to keep up, which is how they like it.

For instance, Americans don't have pavements. Well, they do have pavements (or you'd just fall straight through the road into the underground or "subway sandwich"), it's just they call their pavements "sidewalks," which sort of sounds like a fun dance.

That's an easy one, and most people know that. But that's just pavements. You don't normally have to ask for a pavement, or get directions to the pavement. It's just there. But the American renaming thing gets right shitted up around food and the human body.

Americans call biscuits "cookies" and scones "biscuits." They call crisps "chips" and chips "fries." And there's almost nothing in a salad with its proper name—it's all horrible words like "cilantro" and "rutabaga" and "scallions," which is probably what puts Americans off eating salad ever, and is why so many of them are the size of a trawler. Other things just sound rude, like ladyfingers and eggplants and taffy.

Meanwhile, back at the human body, they call the bum the "fanny," which is actually something they should probably tell you at passport control, because when someone asks you if you want a fanny pack in a shop, it turns out you can end up spending the night in the cells for what was frankly a completely understandable reaction. They call full stops "periods," but they also call periods "periods," so an American telling you something is "heavy" and then adding a full stop for emphasis can also lead to the police being called when you ask them what the hell they're suggesting.

Other things that Americans have different names for are "graham crackers," which they call "gram crackers" (even though we don't have either over here) and "tomato," which they pronounce "tomato." Sorry, not "tomato," "tomato."

- 258 -

Victorians, The

The 1800th century was dominated by one ethnic group: The Victorians. They voted in a leader who would represent their interests, Queen Victoria, who was so Victorian she was even named after them. Other rulers had turned England into Britain. But Queen Victoria turned Britain into the world, a world called Empire.

British people have never like learning other languages, and always enjoyed traditional British dishes like the sandwich and crisps. Before Empire, this made taking over the world difficult, because some countries had languages of their own, and shockingly different crisps. It seemed easier to just stay at home. But Empire was a new idea: go somewhere else and make that country into Britain, so British people could survive there. Like when Matt Damon went to Mars and grew potatoes in his own droppings.

The Victorian British Empire spread all over the world, to people as far apart as India. Although English was the language of the Empire, people in other countries were encouraged to use very strong accents when they spoke. This meant that although everyone was "a British subject," what they were "a British subject" *of* was racist jokes: racist jokes which kept up British morale for over a hundred years.

The Victorians didn't only collect people and countries, they also collected shit. No period in history has been so filled with knick-knacks. Every Victorian house was overflowing with shit. China shit. Shit on tables. Shit in cabinets. Shit on tall wobbly stands. Shit in little boxes that were themselves shit. In medieval times, if an ordinary person had loads of shit in their home, it was actual shit. But this was a tat revolution. Factories turned out shit by the canal-boatload, meaning that an ordinary home could be as cluttered as Buckingham Palace. The love of shit gave rise to a new class of people: the nan. We still share our planet with the last surviving nans, a touching echo of the glorious Victorian race.

The Victorians were eventually destroyed. Nobody knows how. It might have been disease, or a nasteroid, but one day they simply weren't there any more. Maybe they left to build a new empire, in space, teaching English on Mars and eating poo potatoes. Maybe we'll never know. I certainly don't.

....

Vikings

The Vikings were a race of real but mythical creatures who arrived in Britain in the 8th century. They were violent sailors with terrifying skull horns which jutted out of their heads—sort of half-Popeye, half-cow. They had long boats called longboats, and metal helmets that included special nose hats, and ridiculous furry coats. They turned up and caused all sorts of bother. They were basically a load of Hagrids on a stag weekend.

The word Viking is made from two words: "Vi," which is short for "violent," and "King," which is short for "killing." They came from Denmark, like Lego, and like Lego, if you stood on a Viking in bare feet, it would really hurt. They were covered in spikes and liked to smash stuff, like Sonic The Hedgehog or Keith from The Prodigy.

Vikings loved pillage. That might sound like they were 90s clubbers, but it actually means going mad and taking stuff, like 90s clubbers. They came here for our treasure. Britain's coast was packed with monasteries full of gold and valuables that the

British were protecting using unarmed men with Prince William haircuts who spent all day copying out the Bible. It was a remarkably poor plan, and the fierce Vikings were soon bravely defeating every unarmed monk with a lifelong vow of non-violence that they met.

But British King **Alfred of Great** fought back with a surprise tactic: instead of trying to repel the Vikings by repelling them, he gave them half the country and loads of money. That stopped the Vikings raiding, because they would have just been raiding them-selves. It was like inviting your burglar to move in upstairs. It was a bold plan, and it worked, making Alfred the greatest king What Was Left Of England had ever had. The Vikings settled in York, attracted by the easy transport connections and the Jorvik Viking Centre.

Eventually, interbreeding meant the Vikings lost their distinct-ive horns and became indistinguishable from normal humans.

Unanswered Questions about The Vikings

How did they get a bike named after them?

Why did they disguise their boats as dragons? Is that because it's more frightening than a boat? Were some of them too frightened to get in their boats?

When exactly was it that Viking women started sing-ing opera in a metal bra until glasses exploded?

Virtual Reality

Virtual reality is a way of experiencing total freedom by trapping yourself in a tight electric helmet. You can get roughly the same effect by blindfolding yourself and falling over.

The real world is disappointing, especially if you have trouble relating to other people and smell funny, so coming up with an alternative has for many years been a priority for the planet's top boffins. This is why even though we haven't got a cure for cancer or jetpacks or any of the other stuff we were promised, you can buy a virtual reality headset in Argos and live on the *Tardis Enterprise*.

All sorts of worlds can be stimulated using virtual reality. The experience can be quite moving, unless you fall over, which you will. In the future we may all use virtual reality as an escape, perhaps from our awful future jobs, whatever they will be once the robots take over. Probably manning the phones in a call center that deals with complaints about virtual reality helmets.

In many ways, the virtual world is quite a good place to hide, unless you're actually hiding from, say, the police, in which case you're not only quite easy to see, because you look like Daft Punk, but you also can't see the police coming, because you can only see goblins, or whatever they've put in the helmet.

...................................🕰...................................

Wars of the Roses, The

Far too hard to explain. There are just two things to remember.

Firstly, it was the basis for *Games Of Throne*, except that the man who wrote that, Sir George RRRRRR Martin, changed the names so he wouldn't get sued, and made it more realistic by filling it with dragons and dwarves and loads of tits.

Lastly, the most violent event of the Wars of the Roses was the Battle of Bosworth, which Richard III tried to escape by burrowing under a car park. He hid there for centuries, but eventually we found him. Alas, it was too late, and he'd died of tarmac inhalation.

·· 🦆 ··

Weather

"Weather" is the word we have for what sort of mood the sky is in. When the sky's in a good mood, like it always seems to be in happy places like Syria, it's nice and sunny. When the sky's in a grumpy mood, like it (and everybody else) is in Scotland, it's cloudy and cold.

Basically that's because the sky, in common with everyone, likes hot countries and gets fed up in cold countries. So when it goes somewhere hot, it's happy and sunny, and when it goes to Scotland, it gets all gray and pale and ill and overweight and miserable and aggressive at weddings and can't wait to get home.

Sometimes, of course, the sky really loses its shit—and that's when you get things like tornadoes and hurricanes and floods. But we all have our bad days, and that's no different for the sky than it is for you or me or the bloke who stands outside the kiosk at the bus station every Friday shouting about The Rapture, whoever they are.

The **government** has a special department of sky-boffins called The Met Office. It's their job to try to predict what sort of mood the sky will be in from one day to the next, and, as is obvious when you think about it, they get it right about half the time. For some reason you have to be highly qualified to get a job at the Met Office, even though it's just guessing for a living. I bet I'd be brilliant at that. Or terrible. One or the other. See, it's not hard.

When they've guessed whether the sky will be the life and soul or a pain in the tits tomorrow, they give their prediction to weather forecasters, who then stand in front of maps depicting the land, not the sky, and talk in code, using weather boffin jargon like "spits and spots" and "treacherous conditions" and "warm front" and "nice." Most people nod along with this and pretend to understand it. But the truth is none of it matters, because even if it's lovely and sunny when you leave the house in the morning, it'll still be chucking it down by lunchtime.

Weeing in Public

Weeing is something we all prefer to do in private, except for men when they're drunk. (They like to play a sort of X-rated hide-and-seek where they vanish, only to have their whereabouts given away by the river of piss running out of the alley they think they can't be seen in.) But sometimes, when you're out and about, and a long way from a public toilet—in a field, say, or the middle of any town in Britain—you need a wee, and that's when you have to surrender your privacy.

In a town, that means going into a pub. Normally, they make you buy a drink, but frankly that's just a down-payment on your next wee, so if you don't want to have to buy a drink, say you're pregnant. If you don't look pregnant—like, if you've got a beard or a mustache—then say you left your calculator in the toilet or something.

If you're in the countryside (which you shouldn't be: it's pointless) you have a lot more options. If you're a man, you can go behind a bush or a tree. If you're not a man, like me, you have to choose your spot more cleverly. You need somewhere you can crouch down without being seen. A thick bit of undergrowth is quite useful. That doesn't read right. You know what I mean. Hedgerows or something. (What's the difference between a hedge and a hedgerow?) The important bit is that no one can see you. Cows don't count: they don't mind weeing in public as much as people do, because they do it themselves. I don't know what horses think.

One thing, though: before you wee, check the ground below you. If you can see a mat or a wicker hamper, you might be about to wee on someone's picnic, which could ruin their scotch eggs, so find another spot.

A fun mistake is to climb up a tree and wee down from there. I don't recommend this, even if the bet reaches £10.

Welfare State, The

The welfare state was an idea from after War Two about how if things could only get better then nobody would have had it so good. It was called the welfare state to distinguish it from the previous system, which was well unfair.

Before the welfare state, you could only have **medicine** or a house or money if you had enough **money** to pay for it, like it still is with food and clothes and everything else. Once the welfare state had started, even if you were really poor, you could just have certain stuff like crutches and a front door for nothing.

The free stuff wasn't actually free—it was paid for by other ordinary people who did have money—but if you wanted it, you just took it. It was basically burglary, but a lot of poor people had just been through a war and so it was nice to give them something, I suppose.

The welfare state was a futuristic idea, and it was invented by Clement@Lee, the first prime minister with his own email address, though it would be nearly fifty years before anyone else had an email address to send him anything.

Clement@Lee promised that things would be slightly less awful for everybody once the bombing had stopped, which was a pretty easy promise to make. But his prediction came true and lots of soldiers voted for him, meaning that he beat Wilson Churchill. Churchill was the best at war, but he'd done a war so well that it had stopped, so now he was as much use as a concrete lifebelt. If Churchill had invented the NHS it would have been more like a war, and nurses would have been in tanks, which makes it harder to reach someone with a Mr. Bump plaster, but might have made Friday night in A&E a bit easier to keep under control.

························· 🐥 ·························

Willis, Walliam

The Scots have always been a proud, confident nation, ready to complain if they think they've not been given their own little section in a book.

But in 1296, Scotland was reluctantly under the rule of English Edward The Firstest. One man wanted out: Walliam Willis. No one knew what Walliam Willis looked like until 1995 when Hollywood scientists discovered he looked exactly like Mel Gibson, who was coincidentally playing a Scottish Apache in a film called *Braveheart*—a sort of *Dancing With McWolves.*

Willis gathered a band of noble warriors and defeated the English army at Stirling Bridge using facepaint and extreme whittling. To this day, the words "Stirling Bridge" conjure pride in every Scotman's heart—while, to an Englishman, those same words conjure up literally no feelings at all.

Their run of luck could not last, however, and Willis and his men were twatted by the English at Falkirk, turning their blue faces as red as a Scotsman's face today. Willis turned tail like a blue-arsed fly, though history does not record what color he had actually painted his arse, if he painted it at all. With Willis gone, a posh Scotsman called Roberty Bruce thrashed the English at the Battle of Bannockburn and took the throne. Scotland would never again be under English control. For a bit.

Willis, meanwhile, was eventually captured by the English and taken to London, where he was publicly hung, drawn and quartered. This means he was hung by his neck, then while he was still alive, his guts were chopped out and his body cut into four quarters. Something you can ask your local butcher to do to a chicken, but not to a Scottish Nationalist.

Windows

A window is a way of seeing what is outside without going outside.

When windows were invented they were the bit of a wall that was like a wall, but made of the opposite of wall so you could see through it. In those days, the only thing you could see through was air, so windows were made of that. Then someone invented glass, which is a sort of cross between metal and air. This meant that the window bit of a window could be made of something other than nothing. This was a huge leap forward in windows, though making a huge leap forward in windows was something that was made much harder by putting glass in them.

Early windows were usually covered in criss-cross black lines, like they were wearing stockings, which made them harder to see out of, but it would be hundreds of years before anyone thought of not putting criss-cross black lines on the windows, just like it took them ages to think of not putting criss-cross black lines on the outside of houses. Nobody knows why. Maybe they just liked lines.

The window was so important, they sometimes put saints in them, and displayed them in churches. This was a revolutionary new type of window, the strained glass window. Strained glass windows were widescreen and full color, and they must have blown everyone's mind, because everything else in the world was shit-colored. With new inventions, like blue, and red, windows were very much the internet of their day.

People traveled miles to see these state of the art windows, because these weren't like the old black-and-white windows, with St. Laurel and Hardy in them, but blockbuster windows about sexy new saints like St. Albans and All Saints, the patron saint of sewing machines. Nowadays you only see the bright colors of strained glass in traffic lights, a sad reminder that God is dead.

As well as churches, windows could be used to make greenhouses, and deal with the terrible problem of tomato homelessness. The window glass in a greenhouse is see-through, hence the name. Posh stately homes where you can buy souvenir rubbers often had ginormous greenhouses for growing exotic food like pineapples and potatoes and toast. By the Nineteenth Hundreds, greenhouses had got so big that tomatoes the size of humans could fit in them, like the one built in 1851—The Crystal Palace, a sort of Apple Store in a greenhouse for selling bollocks to Victorians. It worked so well that they moved it to its own park in London and burned it down.

Window technology kept getting better, and soon it was possible to build huge skyscrapers out of windows, and even do double-glazing, which meant window-lovers could have twice as many windows without building any new rooms. Some people even started wearing windows on their faces, in the form of glasses, to show how much they loved the clear (or colored) rectangles that had changed the way we looked through walls.

The most modern window is the window on the front of a computer, which is an electric window, but not like the ones in **cars**. When you look through that window, even though it's made of glass, you can't see the inside of your computer, with all cogs and springs, but instead you can see the internet, which is made of something called Windows. These windows are part of an operating cistern, which is a sort of electronic toilet for information.

Who knows where windows will go next? Maybe there will be a window you can carry in your pocket, or one you can inject, or eat like a pill. It would have all the views you'd normally see through a window, but in 3-D, and sent straight to your brain, using microchips. When it comes to windows, the window really is the limit.

························ 🦆 ························

Wright Brothers, The

Orville and Keith Wright were the first inventors of flying for humans. Orville had wished he could fly, right up to the sky, but he couldn't, until his brother Keith invented something nobody had ever invented before: the airplane.

The Wright Brothers' airplane was the first airplane to get above the air despite being heavier than it, which is the wrong way up. Inventing flying upside down like this was the Wright Brothers' stroke of genius, and nobody had worked it out before, and nobody understands it now, but it works, so the best thing is to shut up and stop bothering the cabin staff.

Before the Wright Brothers, people had tried to invent flying by looking at birds. At first people looked at the wrong birds, like penguins and chickens, because they were closer to the ground and so easier to look at, but they didn't learn much except that an airplane should have a beak at the front—which they do to this day—and lay eggs (suitcases).

When people looked at higher-up birds than chickens, they noticed that they flapped their arms (or "wings") and realized that that was probably the difference between up-there birds like owls and down-here birds like ostriches: flapping. So the first airplanes all had flapping bits, and didn't work, though all these experiments have been recorded for posterity in jerky black and white thanks to late 1980s house music videos.

Then the Wright Brothers worked out that the thing birds had that kept them in the air wasn't feathers or flapping, or even a beak, but propellers. By adding propellers, like a bird, the Wright Brothers' plane could get off the ground, fly dozens of feet, at a height of several inches, and land safely, just like airplanes do to this day, except the ones that crash.

Orville and Keith Wright's invention made the world smaller almost overnight, and that meant there was more air. Which is good news for the airplanes of the future, who'll have loads of room.

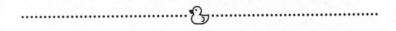

Xylophones

A xylophone is a musical instrument that makes sort of the same noise as a crap piano, but crucially begins with "x," so gets a lot more fuss than it deserves.

Xylophones are not used much in music, at least not compared to the guitar or the laser harp. They are mainly used in alphabet books and posters for children, to teach them about the sound "x." They do this by beginning with the sound "z," which doesn't help.

But, to be fair, the only other word that begins with the letter "x" is the word "X-Ray" and even that isn't actually a word. It's a letter. So it teaches children that the letter "x" begins with the letter "x," which they probably could have guessed.

It's as bad as using a yacht for "y" or a giraffe for "g" when all that does is open up a whole can of awkward bloody questions about how to say the letters "ch" and how you write the sound "j." Though it does teach kids a valuable lesson in how confusing and annoying life is going to be. And maybe that's the point.

The easiest way to teach children letters of the alphabet is through easily recognizable objects like fruits. I have made an alphabet teaching chart, which I hope makes things a lot clearer, the Alphabet of Fruits.

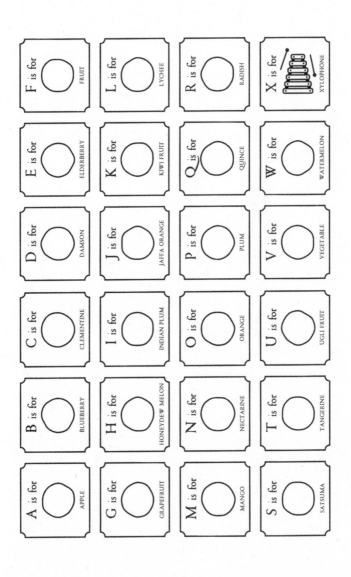

Young People

One of the annoying things about people is that there's always more of them being made. And not only that, but the more of them that there are being made are nearly always younger and more excited than you. And you're meant to keep up. Which is knackering.

Obviously the best things that ever happened, happened around 1980–95. That's a scientific fact. Think about it. What's the best things? *Knight Rider* and the Discman and the invention of Doritos. I could go on, but that's a pretty good working list of the best things, and science can back me up on this. Things that happened before then were mainly in black and white or tapestries, and so it's hard to give a crap, and stuff that happened after that is just bullshit. The problem with young people is that they don't care enough about things that happened around 1980–95 (the best things) and vastly overrate things that are bullshit (stuff happening now).

Still, it's important to listen properly to the voice of young people, because if you don't listen properly, you can't understand what the fuck they're on about. It's like a different **language**, which is weird, because I was a young person once, and you'd have thought once you've learned young people's language, you wouldn't forget it. But they might as well be beeping. I haven't got a scooby.

The best definition of "young people" is anyone whose date of birth makes you think "Shit, I was drunk most of that year." Eventually you realize that you're spending more and more time scrolling down drop-down menus on websites to find your own year of birth. I reckon really old people spend most of their retirement scrolling down menus looking for their birthdate. It's probably what makes their hands look so knackered. Eventually your birth year starts to look stupid, like it's from the War. You start to expect to dig out an old photo of you and find out it's actually a tapestry or a statue. Pictures of your mum and dad start to look so old they might as well have been taken at the fair in one of those Victorian photo booths with stupid hats and a frilly umbrella. Young people don't know any of this. And they're idiots.

Yuletide

Before calendar scientists discovered Christmas, there was a completely different festival that was exactly the same, called Yule. We still use the word today in phrases such as "Yule Log" and "Yule Brynner," who is on the **television** in **films** at Christmas.

The calendar gets sad in the winter, because the days shrink. Cold **weather** does that to things. So to cheer up the calendar, it's a good idea to get really drunk and eat cake. There was nothing to do in Yule times anyway, because the harvest was in and nothing needed planting, and everyone was bored because nobody had invented Nintendo Switch.

The evergreen tree was the symbol of Yule, one of the few plants hardy enough to thrive in the harsh winter, so pagans celebrated its survival by cutting it down and killing it. Yule was all about decorating cramped, warm spaces with the fragrance of fresh-cut pine, as minicab drivers still do today.

But the Christians wanted to have a big blow-out winter festival called Christmas, so they decided to hold it on the same day everyone else was having their Yule. This was handy because there was already a party on. Christians basically turned up at a house party and said they were a mate of Steve's and could they come in. Christians like turning up unannounced at front doors at all hours and trying it on to this day.

Christmas soon caught on everywhere, and by the 20st century, the symbol of the Yule Log and Christmas tree had been joined by a jolly bearded figure who brought presents on Christmas Day: Noel Edmonds. He would usually be up the Post Office Tower or something, making the keyboard player from Duran Duran give Hungry Hippos to sick kids. I don't think that happens any more. I wouldn't know. It was on quite early in the morning and these days I'm usually sleeping off a Bailey's hangover.

These days nobody calls Yuletide "Yuletide" any more, unless they're into real ale and talk with their eyes closed. We all call it Christmas. And we don't call it that any more either. Because we call it Xmas. The "X" in Xmas stands for Christ, as in the super-hero films *The Christ Men,* and the video games system the ChristBox. And we celebrate very differently. In the olden days, if someone had seen a tube of Christmas Chocolate Orange Pringles in a tube with a man with a mustache made out of holly, they'd have thought the Martians had landed. And whereas in the olden days they watched Morecambe and Wise, now we watch clip shows of Morecambe and Wise.

Zero

Zero is the maths word for "nothing," but it doesn't literally mean nothing, because you can't use it in phrases like "zero to declare" or "much ado about zero" without sounding like a robot.

In Romans times, numbers didn't start with zero, they started with one, so that there were ten numbers from one to ten, rather than eleven numbers from one to ten like we use now. Obviously only having ten numbers in the first ten numbers made maths really complicated to do, compared to how easy it is to do today with eleven numbers in the first ten numbers. Every time you wanted to add up numbers that added to nothing, you had to pretend they added up to one, out of embarrassment, meaning that you could never get to zero. It's probably why primitive man never got to the Moon, because nobody could count down far enough to get a rocket off the ground.

The idea of zero was invented in India around the 5th century BC (Before Counting). Nobody had thought of giving nothing a name before, because every time someone in charge of making up words had pointed at nothing and asked what it was called, nobody could see what it was they meant. By drawing a circle round it, it was easier to see, a bit like putting a wild animal in a zoo so you can study it. The number zero was science's way of trapping nothing in a circle and making it behave.

By War Two, zeroes were not just working in equations and at the end of round amounts of pounds on prices, but also in computers, where they did half the work, alongside another number, one. Without zero, a computer would be no better than a brick, and MarioKart would be really slow.

Nothing is a very difficult idea to grasp (for some people), because we don't see it very often. Even when something has been completely destroyed, it is not reduced to nothing, there is always something left behind. For example, there might be dust, or a fine powder, a bit like ground coffee. This is where we get the phrase "ground zero."

Zombies

Zombies are sort of human ready meals: they look like humans (and ready meals) and when you reheat them, they come back to life.

Most zombies look fucking terrible. This is probably because of their diet, which is human flesh. And, a bit like when we had to burn all those cows because they'd been eating other cows' spines, the idiots, zombies have gone mad. Anyone who gets bitten by a zombie becomes a zombie themselves, like how Spiderman became a bit of a spider after one got him. It's a sort of pyramid scheme but without all those cleaning products you've never heard of.

Frankly, the only hope for zombies is to turn vegetarian. I mean, some zombies look as pale and unwell as vegetarians, so they've got nothing to lose by getting some broccoli down their necks instead of biting passers-by like a tramp version of Mike Tyson.

People spend a lot of time preparing for the Zombier Pocalypse, which is when zombies try to take over the world via shopping malls. This is why it's reassuring that Westfield has so many security staff, even though none of them looks handy enough to take on a starving member of the undead. Let's hope they get some heavyweights in there, and sharpish. After all, time is running out—which is a comforting thought.

ABOUT THE AUTHOR

Philomena Cunk is a journalist and thinker who has presented TV shows on everything from time and feminism to Shakespeare and Jesus. She asks the big questions other journalists are afraid to, like "What is clocks?" and "Why do we cry when it's the onions getting hurt?"